**This glossory is for:** 1) folks who like a little guidance, and 2) folks who have been personally victimized by the phrase "season to taste." So, before we get into these recipes, let's all agree on one thing: Precision is lovely, but flavor is the goal. Welcome to the South—where "a dash" is both a measurement and a spiritual suggestion.

## THE MEASUREMENTS

**A Tad/A Bit**
About ¼ teaspoon

**A Dash**
A quick flick of the wrist—roughly ⅛ teaspoon

**A Pinch**
What fits between your thumb and forefinger—about 1/16 teaspoon

**A Smidgen**
Even less than a pinch—about 1/32 teaspoon *(It's also known as: "Just enough to make you feel responsible.")*

**A Cracklin' (of Pepper)**
A few confident turns of the pepper grinder—enough to see it, smell it, and feel slightly powerful—roughly to ¼ teaspoon, depending on how strong your wrist is at the moment

**A Whisper**
Barely there, the amount you add when you're trying not to offend somebody's blood pressure

**A Shake**
One good shake from the seasoning bottle *(If the lid is loose, that becomes a testimony.)*

**A Couple Shakes**
Two to four shakes *(This is where recipes start getting personal.)*

**A Sprinkle**
A light scatter across the top—usually ½ to 1 teaspoon

**A Dusting**
Even lighter than a sprinkle, enough to look pretty, but not enough to cough

**A Shower**
A generous sprinkle, often applied to cheese. *(If you can still see what's underneath, keep going.)*

**A Blanket of Cheese**
When you can no longer identify the original dish by sight, this is correct

**A Dollop**
A spoonful of something soft like sour cream, whipped cream, or mayo—about ½ to 1 tablespoon

**A Knob of Butter**
A chunk about the size of your thumb—roughly 1 to 2 tablespoons

**A Pat of Butter**
A thin slice—about 1 tablespoon *(Unless Mamaw is watching, then a "pat" is the size of a paperback book.)*

**A Stick**
Southern Standard Unit = ½ cup butter *(Also, it's a lifestyle.)*

**A Handful**
What fits in your cupped hand—about ¼ cup *(If you've got farmer hands, it's ½ cup and nobody argues.)*

**A Palmful**
A flatter handful, slightly less than a full handful *(This is "I'm being careful," Southern edition.)*

**A Swirl**
One slow circle around the pan—the addition of sauce, honey, or syrup—usually 1 to 2 tablespoons

**A Drizzle**
A thinner swirl, the amount you use when you're pretending to be delicate

**A Splash**
A small amount of liquid—often 1 to 3 teaspoons

**A Sploosh**
More than a splash, less than a pour, usually happens when you get distracted mid-sentence

**A Glug**
Enough oil to slick a skillet

**A Pour**
A steady stream for 1 to 2 seconds

**A Heavy Pour**
A pour that says, "The Lord knows my heart."

## THE GUIDELINES

**"Until it smells right."**
Used for sautéing onions/garlic and blooming spices—trust your nose.

**"Stir 'til it behaves."**
Mix until it stops looking separated and starts looking like it has purpose.

**"A taste and a fix."**
Taste it. Adjust salt, pepper, acid, sweetness—whatever it needs. Repeat until you stop making that squinty face.

**Measure with your heart**
The most important instruction—add seasoning or ingredients until it feels right. *(This means sometimes adding more than you planned, and that's okay.)*

MEGHAN LYNN

# Something Good

## An Unexpected Cookbook *for* Life's Unexpected Moments

83 press®

# Dedication

*To my sweet Seth—thank you for loving me steady, making me feel safe, laughing with me loudly, and helping make our home full of both grace and good food.*

*And to my precious Braden and Brenlynn—y'all are my greatest joys, my loudest audience, and the reasons I keep making "just one more" batch. I love you dearly, and I am so proud of you both.*

Published by 83 Press,
an imprint of Hoffman Media, LLC
2323 2nd Avenue North
Birmingham, Alabama 35203
*83press.com*

ISBN 978-1-971708-07-2
Printed in USA

# Contents

# Introduction

*Well, hey!* Welcome to my brightly lit little corner of the world—where we blend the sweet and the savory parts of life into one glorious, slightly chaotic concoction of recipes, lifestyle tips, and the kind of inspiration that tends to show up right on time. If you've ever stood over a stove thinking, *How do people turn a simple meal into a memory?*—honey, you're home.

Because this isn't just a cookbook; it's a celebration of real life. It's the kind of life that gathers folks around the table and serves up not only food, but laughter, stories, and a few good-natured eye rolls when somebody says, "I didn't know you could cook like this." Yes, you did. You just didn't believe. And that's okay. We forgive. We grow.

Cooking is a bit of a dance, and I don't mean the elegant kind with ballroom lessons and posture. I mean the kind where you're holding a hot pan with one hand, stirring with the other, and trying not to trip over a dog who has chosen to lie directly in the path of your dreams.

Some days you lead. Some days you step on your own toes. And some days you end up on the kitchen floor with flour on your face and your pride in the trash can. But that's the beauty of it, isn't it? The kitchen has a way of reminding us we don't have to be perfect to be present. You don't need a spotless house, a curated pantry, or matching cookware to feed people well. You just need a willing heart, a little bit of butter, and the ability to laugh when things go sideways—which, they will.

In these pages, you'll find recipes that feel like a warm hug from Mamaw or Mawmaw—I was lucky enough to have one of each—comforting, familiar, and just a little bit bossy. You'll find flavors bright as a Southern summer garden in full bloom, and dishes that taste like somebody loved you on purpose.

And tucked right in between the recipes, you're gonna find pieces of my life—hilarious mishaps, tender moments, and the lessons I learned right in the middle of ordinary days. The kind of lessons that don't look like much from the outside until I realized they were shaping me the whole time. Because food isn't just food in my world. It's a love language. It's an apology. It's a celebration. It's what you make when you don't know what else to do—so you do the one thing you can do: you feed people.

So, grab your favorite drink, kick off your shoes, and come on in. Whether you're a seasoned cook or someone who once mistook salt for sugar (we are not here to shame—we are here to heal), I promise you're gonna find something that meets you right where you are. Around here, every recipe has a story, and every story has a recipe for a life well-lived. Alright. Let's get into it!

# I Loathe Luci

Meet Luci—and before you clutch your pearls, no, she is not quite *that* Luci . . . but she is absolutely related to the same nonsense. If you've been around me on social media for any length of time, you've probably seen my "I Loathe Luci" series, where this cute, sarcastic, wildly naïve little character shows up with a straight face and the audacity of a thousand demons. Luci is my comedic way of giving the "enemy" a name, a personality, and a voice—because sometimes it's easier to recognize what you're up against when it stops feeling like a vague dark cloud and starts sounding like a very confident liar with good eyeliner.

Luci represents the enemy we face as Christ-followers—those everyday whispers of doubt, distraction, shame, and "are you *sure* God said that?" They try to slide into our minds when we're tired, overwhelmed, or just trying to make it through a generic weekday. And listen, most of us are not out here walking around with a seminary degree in our back pocket, ready to battle spiritual warfare before we've even had our coffee. So, I created Luci on purpose—to make Biblical truth easier to swallow, easier to remember, and honestly . . . easier to smile at. Because sometimes the best way to disarm a lie is to drag it out of the shadows, into the light, and call it for what it is with a smile on your face.

In my social media skits, Luci is always getting into trouble, wandering into sketchy situations, acting confused by earthlings, like she just got dropped off here with no instructions. She's skeptical, dramatic, and fully committed to being wrong with confidence—until truth shows up and shuts the whole thing down. She's comedic relief, yes, but she's also a reminder: The enemy is real, but so is God. And if Luci's presence makes you laugh *and* makes you stronger, then she's doing exactly what I created her to do.

# 1

# Welcome To My Kitchen

This first chapter is where we pull up a chair and get acquainted. Before we get too fancy, before we start acting like we know how to use a mandoline without supervision, we begin where all good things begin: in the kitchen. This chapter is full of the kind of food and stories that built me. This chapter is about home. The homes we grow up in, the homes we build, the recipes that follow us from one season to the next, and the way food can carry love long after the moment has passed. So wash your hands, watch your fingers, and come on in. We're starting at the beginning.

# Welcome To My Kitchen

Not the spotless, show-home, never-been-cooked-in kind of kitchen. I mean MY kitchen—the real one: The kitchen where the counters somehow collect crumbs five seconds after I wipe them. The kitchen where a chair is always pulled out, ready for someone to sit in it and immediately feel relaxed. The kitchen that has held more prayers than some church pews and has also heard more laughter than any comedy show could produce.

My kitchen is not just where I make food. It's where I make sense of life.

Because life is a lot. It's loud. It's complicated. It's tender. It's wild. It's beautiful. And if you're anything like me, sometimes you don't know what to do with all of it—until you have something to do with your hands.

That's what cooking has always been for me. It's a way to turn feelings into something tangible. It's a way to take love—that invisible, impossible-to-measure thing—and put it on a plate where people can actually taste it. Around here, food is our love language. It's our apology. It's our celebration. It's our "I didn't know what to say, so I made you something warm."

My grandparents understood that. My parents did, too. I come from a long line of people who didn't always have perfect words, but they knew how to show up with a casserole. People who could take an ordinary Tuesday and make it feel like comfort just by frying something in a pan and calling you to the table. People who believed that if you fed someone well, you were doing more than filling their stomach—you were also filling a space in their heart that needed care.

And somewhere along the way, I became that kind of person, too. If you've found me online, you already know my kitchen is where I do a lot of my living. It's where I'm funny when I'm trying not to cry. It's where I can make a joke about a cracklin' of pepper, and then turn around and tell you something that sits in your chest for the rest of the day. That's not calculated—it's just honest. That's the truth of being human. We can be laughing at the same time we're hurting. We can be making dessert while our heart is heavy. Both things can be true.

And that's exactly why I have written this book the way I have. I didn't want to give you a cookbook that just tells you what to do and moves on. I wanted to give you a kitchen you could step into. I wanted you to feel what I feel when I cook: that every recipe comes from somewhere. Every dish has a history. Every flavor has a face attached to it. Sometimes, it's a person you love. Sometimes, it's a season you survived. Sometimes, it's a moment you never want to forget. Because food doesn't just taste like food.

It tastes like Friday mornings at Hardee's with my Papaw, when "breakfast dessert" was a cinnamon-raisin biscuit we split inside a paperboard clamshell like it was fine china. It tastes like theater nights and half-priced appetizers and friendships that formed under stage lights. It tastes like hurricanes, when the world outside was absolute chaos but we still needed dinner—and somehow dinner made everything feel a little more secure. It tastes like the day that somebody famous stitched my recipe video, and I about threw my phone into the couch cushions from pure shock. It tastes like grief, too—the kind you carry quietly while you keep feeding people anyway.

These stories aren't extra. They're the ingredient list you can't write down.

They're the "why" behind the "what."

They're the proof that a recipe is never just a recipe. It's a memory you can recreate, a tradition you can keep alive, and a way to say, "You belong here," even if it's your first time at the table.

So, as you flip through these pages, I hope you're going to laugh with me. You'll probably even roll your eyes at me at least once. You might even get a lump in your throat in the middle of a chapter, and then immediately turn the page and find yourself making a casserole like nothing happened—which, honestly, is exactly how life works.

You don't have to be an expert to cook from this book. You don't have to have the prettiest kitchen, the nicest dishes, or a pantry that looks like a magazine. You just need a willingness to show up. To try. To stir. To taste. To learn. To feed someone you love—even if that someone is YOU.

This is your invitation to slow down for a minute, to put your phone face down, and to stand at the counter and let the smell of whatever you're cooking remind you that you're here, you're living, and you're allowed to make ordinary days feel meaningful. Because in my world, the kitchen is where stories get told, where people get cared for, and where love becomes something you can pass across the table.

So, come on in. Tie on an apron. Kick off your shoes. Pull up a chair. Taste as you go, and don't worry if it isn't perfect. In this kitchen, perfection has never been the point. Presence is. Now—let's cook something and make a memory.

# Mamaw's Fried Chicken

SERVES 6 TO 8

**prep:** 20 minutes *(plus 24-hour marinating)* | **cook:** 20 to 25 minutes | **total:** 24 hours 45 minutes

*Mamaw didn't do complicated. She did correct. And her fried chicken is proof that the simplest recipes, done the right way, will beat a fancy one every time. The secret isn't a hundred spices. The secret is time. That 24-hour buttermilk soak changes everything. Don't skip it. I'm begging you.*

- **1 package boneless, skinless chicken thighs (about 2 to 2½ pounds)**
- **Buttermilk, enough to fully submerge the chicken (about 2 to 3 cups)**
- **Peanut oil, for frying (or vegetable oil, but peanut oil is the gold standard)**
- **Self-rising flour (about 2 cups, plus more as needed)**
- **Seasoning salt, to taste**
- **Regular salt, to taste**
- **Garnish: fresh parsley, lemon slices and wedges**

**1. Marinate the chicken. (Don't you dare skip this!).** Place the chicken pieces in a bowl or resealable plastic bag and pour the buttermilk over them until fully submerged. Cover and refrigerate for 24 hours. This is not optional. This is the difference between "good" and "Mamaw-level."

**2. Heat the oil.** When you're ready to fry, pour the peanut oil into a heavy skillet (cast iron preferred) until it's about ½-inch deep. Heat over medium-high until the oil is hot. (Drop a little flour in. If it sizzles, it's ready.)

**3. Mix your dredge.** In a shallow dish, whisk together the self-rising flour, seasoning salt, and regular salt. There's no exact measurement here because Mamaw didn't measure—she knew. Start light and adjust as you go.

**4. Dredge and fry.** Remove the chicken from the buttermilk and let the excess drip off. Dredge each piece in the seasoned flour mixture, coating well. Carefully place the chicken into the hot oil. Do not crowd the pan. Fry in batches. Fry until golden brown and cooked through (when a digital thermometer inserted reaches 165°), flipping as needed, about 6 minutes per side depending on thickness.

**5. Drain and rest.** Transfer the fried chicken to a wire rack or paper towel–lined plate to drain. Let it rest a few minutes before serving. Garnish with parsley and lemon, if desired.

## Kitchen Tips

- Don't rush heating the oil. Too cool = greasy chicken. Too hot = burnt outside, raw inside.
- Fry in batches. Crowding lowers the oil temp and makes the coating sad.
- Self-rising flour is key. It gives you that classic Southern crust with just a little lift.
- If you want extra crunch, let dredged chicken sit for 5 minutes before frying so the flour hydrates and clings.
- Best fresh: Fried chicken is a fresh-food ministry.
- Store: Refrigerate leftovers in an airtight container up to 3 days.
- Reheat: Oven or air fryer at 375° until hot and crisp again (microwave = soggy betrayal).

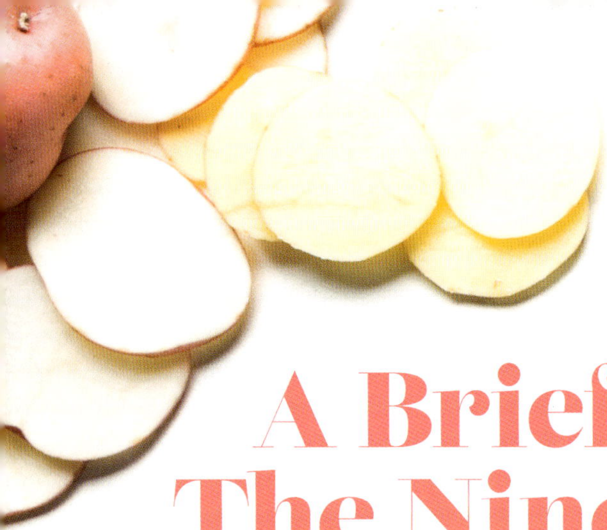

# A Brief Word from The Nine-Finger Chef

Let me gather you close for a moment—because I have a testimony. As I type this, I am doing so with only nine functioning fingers. And before you panic and assume I got into a knife fight over the last biscuit at church, let me clarify: This was not an act of bravery. This was an act of confidence with no guardrail. Literally.

See, we are about to roll right into my au gratin potatoes—an elegant, creamy, cheesy, "Who made this and why are they not running for office?" kind of recipe. And for that casserole, I'm going to recommend you use a mandoline, a slicer that will give you those gorgeous, uniform potato slices that bake evenly and make you feel like you went to culinary school instead of YouTube University. But, beloved . . . a mandoline is not a kitchen tool. A mandoline is a tiny guillotine with a handle, and it does not care about your dreams, your plans, or your level of experience.

One night, I was in my kitchen, minding my business, doing what I always do—turning potatoes into something magical. I had my mandoline out, feeling efficient. Feeling professional. Feeling like the kind of woman who does not need instructions, because I have made casseroles in high-pressure environments. I have cooked through storms. I have hosted parties in monsoons. I have survived hot honey and high expectations.

So naturally, I did what every overly confident grown woman does: I did not use the guard. Because why would I use the guard? I'm a seasoned pro. I have thumbs. I have reflexes. I have . . . audacity. And then I reached the last potato. Now listen—one thing about me: I don't like waste. I was raised by people who will scrape the last teaspoon of batter out of a bowl like it's the Great Depression and the Lord is watching. So I'm slicing . . . and slicing . . . and getting closer . . . and closer . . . to the end of that potato.

And I'm thinking, *Just one more slice. Just one more. I can do this.* Friends. The mandoline came down and guillotined the tip of my left ring finger like it was signing up for the French Revolution.

One second, I had 10 fingertips. The next second, I had a potato slice and a spiritual awakening.

And I did not know two things:

1. Fingertips can bleed like they've got a personal vendetta.
2. Fingertips can hurt like a third-grade breakup.

I stood there in the kitchen, staring at my hand like, "*Is this . . . mine?*" while my body tried to decide between "fight," "flight," and "pass out."

So, here is my warning, from one casserole-loving citizen to another: It does not matter if you are a beginner, a professional, or a woman who has said the words, "I can eyeball that," with full confidence. Use the guard. Slow down. Pay attention. Because mandolines are wonderful, but they are also the only kitchen appliance I know that occasionally requires a blood sacrifice to operate properly.

And mine was accepted that night.

So, when you get to these au gratin potatoes, and you pull out your mandoline, hear my voice in your ear like a Southern guardian angel with Band-Aids for wings:

"Use the guard, honey. Don't make it 10 toes down and 9 fingertips deep."

Alright. Now that we've covered safety . . . Let's make something good.

"Use the mandoline guard. Or don't. I love consequences."

—*Luci*

# Fancy Potatoes

SERVES 8 TO 10

**prep:** 25 minutes | **cook:** 1 hour 15 minutes | **total:** 1 hour 50 minutes *(includes resting)*

*Au gratin potatoes are creamy, cheesy, golden on top, and just fancy enough to make folks think you worked harder than you did. The key here is slicing your potatoes evenly so they bake at the same pace. This is where a mandoline earns its keep. If you don't have one, slice carefully and pretend you meant for the rustic look. I support you.*

**Softened butter (for greasing the baking dish)**
**2 pounds Yukon gold potatoes**
**4 tablespoons salted butter**
**1 small shallot, diced**
**1 head garlic, minced (yes, a whole head—trust me)**
**3 tablespoons all-purpose flour**
**2 cups heavy cream**
**1½ cups freshly shredded white Cheddar cheese**
**1½ cups freshly grated Parmesan cheese**
**1 teaspoon garlic powder**
**1 teaspoon smoked paprika**
**2 teaspoons chopped fresh parsley**
**½ teaspoon ground cloves**
**Salt and ground black pepper, to taste**

**1. Preheat and prep.** Preheat your oven to 400°. Generously grease a 3-quart baking dish.

**2. Slice your potatoes.** Slice the potatoes into uniform 1⁄16-inch rounds. You want "thin enough to cook," not "accidentally made into chips."

**3. Arrange the potatoes.** Line the slices up neatly in the baking dish in rows—standing them slightly upright so you get those crispy edges and creamy centers. Don't cram them in like sardines, but don't leave them lonely either.

**4. Start the cream sauce.** In a small saucepan over medium heat, melt the butter. Add the shallot and cook 2 to 3 minutes until softened. Stir in the minced garlic and cook 30 seconds until fragrant.

**5. Build the roux.** Sprinkle in the flour and whisk constantly, cooking 1 to 2 minutes until it smells a little toasty (not burned—this isn't a life lesson today).

**6. Add the cream.** Slowly whisk in the heavy cream. Cook, whisking, until thickened, about 5 minutes.

**7. Melt the cheese and season.** Reduce heat to low. Stir in the white Cheddar, Parmesan, garlic powder, smoked paprika, parsley, cloves, plus salt and pepper to taste. Stir until smooth. Let the sauce cool slightly for 1 to 2 minutes.

**8. Pour and tuck the sauce in.** Pour the sauce over the potatoes. Use a spoon (or your clean fingers, because you're at home) to gently separate the slices so the sauce slips down between the layers. Every potato deserves to be loved and sauced equally. Sprinkle with more pepper, if desired.

**9. Bake in stages.** Cover with foil and bake 45 minutes. Uncover and bake 30 minutes more, until golden, bubbly, and smelling like somebody's about to ask for the recipe.

**10. Rest before serving.** Let it sit 10 minutes so the sauce sets up and the flavor gets its act together.

## Kitchen Tips

* Cheese rule: Shred your own Cheddar. Preshredded is coated in anti-caking agents, and I don't trust that.
* Sauce too thick? Add a splash more cream and whisk until smooth.
* Want extra crispy edges? Arrange potatoes more upright and don't drown the top in sauce—let it breathe a little.
* Make Ahead: Assemble the whole dish (unbaked) up to 1 day ahead. Cover and refrigerate. Add 10 to 15 minutes to the covered bake time if baking straight from cold.
* Storage: Refrigerate leftovers in an airtight container for 3 to 4 days.
* Reheat: Oven is best: 350°, covered, until warmed through (about 15 to 20 minutes). Microwave works too—but you'll lose some of that crisp top.

# The Importane of Mise En Place

Summers in Florida are a full-body experience. The air is so thick with humidity you can practically swim to the mailbox. The sun doesn't "shine" so much as it presses charges. And by about 2:00 p.m., your hair has given up, and your clothes have fused to your skin.

But when you're a kid, none of that matters. Summer feels endless—like the days stretch out on purpose just so you can squeeze in one more bike ride, one more sprinkler run, one more barefoot dash across the yard that ends in a dramatic hop because the sidewalk is basically a frying pan.

And on one such sweltering afternoon, when I was about 8 years old, I burst through my Mawmaw and Pawpaw's screened door like I was escaping danger.

I was flushed from playing outside. My cheeks were red. My limbs were sticky. My soul was thirsty. And I had one singular, all-consuming desire:

An ice cream sundae. Not "a snack." Not "a little treat." A sundae. A towering masterpiece. A culinary monument to childhood freedom. Now Mawmaw and Pawpaw were the reigning queen and king of sundaes. Their house stayed stocked with all the fixin's a kid could dream of—velvety ice cream, chocolate sauce, caramel, whipped cream in a can (which is not just a topping, it's a personality), and enough rainbow sprinkles to make a unicorn jealous.

But the crowning glory—the ruby atop the royal scepter—the thing that turned a bowl of ice cream into a *ceremony* . . . was the maraschino cherry.

So, I went to work with the focus of a master architect. I scooped. I drizzled. I layered. I built a big poof of whipped cream like a cloud the angels themselves would sit on. I was finishing strong.

And then . . . I reached for the cherry. And the jar was nowhere to be found. No red lid. No syrupy glow. No familiar clink of glass. My crown jewel was missing. My sundae—my masterpiece—was suddenly incomplete. I stood there in the kitchen staring at my creation like it had betrayed me.

And just as despair began to take root, I opened the fridge to put away the sauces, and I saw it. A clear plastic box sitting on the top shelf, full of what appeared to be the most perfect, freshest cherries I had ever seen. They were red. Round. Shiny. Plump. They were practically glowing. My brain said, *The Lord provides.*

I hollered for Pawpaw, who was lounging nearby in his armchair, enjoying his peaceful life and not knowing his granddaughter was seconds away from culinary trauma. "Hey, Pawpaw!" I called, voice full of hope. "Can I grab a cherry out of this box in here?"

He glanced over with mild confusion. His eyes squinted a little, like he was trying to remember if we were even a "fresh cherry family."

Then, he shrugged—because Pawpaw's default setting was "sure, why not," and said, "Sure you can!" Bless him. That "sure you can" changed my life. I selected the most magnificent "cherry" in the box—largest one, brightest one, the chosen one—and placed it triumphantly atop my whipped cream peak like I was crowning a queen.

It sat there beautiful and bold, the shining star of my dessert galaxy. I carried that sundae to the couch. I turned on the movie *Sleeping Beauty*. I settled in. I was giddy.

Now, as any serious sundae person knows, the cherry must be included in the first bite. The cherry sets the tone. The cherry blesses the journey. The cherry tells your mouth, "We are about to have a good time."

So, I plunged my spoon through whipped cream, down into the swirl of chocolate ice cream and caramel, scooping up a perfect bite—with the cherry riding on top like it was about to fulfill its destiny. I brought the spoon to my mouth. I bit down with full confidence, and friends, my mouth was violated. Because that was not a cherry. That was a cherry tomato. A whole cherry tomato. An innocent-looking liar.

And when I bit into it, it exploded—watery, seedy, bitter tomato guts gushing across my tongue and mixing with caramel and chocolate like a betrayal smoothie.

It was sweet. Then, it was *not* sweet. Then, it was confusion. Then it was panic. I screamed. I gagged. I spit.

Pawpaw came in like, "What's wrong?!"

And I—between coughing and emotional damage—managed to croak out, "THAT WAS A TOMATO."

He stared at me for a beat . . . and then started laughing. Because of course he did. Pawpaw's laughter was always bubbling right under the surface, and apparently, my suffering was the perfect time for it to boil over.

To this day, I approach any sundae with a sprinkle of skepticism. I side-eye every cherry that crosses my path like, I know what you are capable of.

And honestly? That tiny tragedy taught me one of the most important kitchen lessons I've ever learned—long before I knew the fancy French term for it: Mise en place. It sounds elegant. It sounds like something you say while wearing a linen apron and sipping sparkling water. But what it really means is: Get your crap together before you start.

Check your ingredients. Prep what you need. Make sure the thing you think is a cherry is not, in fact, a tomato that's been sitting in the fridge waiting to humble you.

Because in my desperate, hurried quest for a cherry, I grabbed the first thing that looked right.

And assumptions, honey, are a chef's worst enemy.

Mise en place is the calm before the storm. The moment where you lay everything out—ingredients, measurements, tools—so that when the cooking starts, you're not running around like a headless chicken.

It's not about perfection. It's about peace.

It's about knowing what you have, what you need, and what you're actually working with—before you throw it into the mix and hope for the best.

So, if you take anything from my childhood tomato sundae tragedy, let it be this:

Prep before you panic. And for the love of everything holy . . . double-check your produce.

# Cherry Delight

SERVES ABOUT 12

**prep:** 10 minutes | **cook:** 40 to 50 minutes | **total:** 1 hour to 1 hour 10 minutes *(includes cooling)*

*This is what happens when a dump cake goes to finishing school and comes back wearing pearls. It's sweet, gooey, crunchy on top, and unapologetically extra—in the best way. For maximum joy, serve it with vanilla ice cream or a big ole spoonful of whipped cream.*

- **1 (21-ounce) can cherry pie filling**
- **1 (20-ounce) can crushed unsweetened pineapple, undrained**
- **1 (15.25-ounce) box yellow cake mix**
- **½ cup (1 stick) salted butter, melted**
- **1 cup chopped pecans (or walnuts, but pecans are the correct answer)**
- **1½ cups shredded coconut (sweetened or unsweetened—your choice)**
- **Whipped cream, to serve**

**1. Preheat and grease (if you want).** Preheat your oven to 350°. Grab a 13x9-inch baking dish (grease it if you're nervous, but it's not required).

**2. Put it together.** Layer everything in this exact order—do not stir: cherry pie filling, crushed pineapple (with the juice), dry yellow cake mix (sprinkle evenly), melted butter (drizzle as evenly as you can), chopped pecans, and shredded coconut.

**3. Bake and serve.** Bake for 40 to 50 minutes, or until the top is golden and bubbly and the edges look like they're having a good time. Let it cool for 10 to 15 minutes so it sets up a little. Serve warm with whipped cream.

## Kitchen Tips

* Butter coverage matters: Try to drizzle the butter across the surface so most of the cake mix gets moistened. Dry patches happen—life goes on—but we aim for minimal crusty flour situations.
* Make Ahead: Assemble and bake same day for best texture, but leftovers are still delicious.
* Storage: Cover and refrigerate for up to 4 days.
* Reheat: Warm individual servings in the microwave for 20 to 30 seconds.
* Freeze: Freeze tightly wrapped portions for up to 2 months; thaw overnight in the fridge and warm to serve.

"Sounds suspicious until you taste it, which is how most bad ideas begin."

*—Luci*

# Potato Candy

SERVES ABOUT 20

**prep:** 20 minutes | **cook:** 15 minutes | **total:** 3 hour 35 minutes *(includes chilling)*

*I know. Potato . . . candy? Trust me—this is one of those old-school Southern miracles where something humble turns into something ridiculously good. Soft, sweet, peanut-buttery pinwheels that taste like nostalgia.*

**1 small to medium russet potato (about 6 to 8 ounces), peeled and diced**
**Sprinkle of vanilla extract**
**Dash of salt**
**5 to 6 cups powdered sugar, plus more for dusting**
**½ cup peanut butter (creamy works easiest, but do what your heart says)**

**1. Boil the potato.** Boil the potato in water until fork-tender, about 12 to 15 minutes. Drain well.

**2. Mash it smooth.** Mash the potato until there are no lumps.

**3. Make the dough.** Add the mashed potato to a stand mixer bowl. Mix in the vanilla and salt. With the mixer on low, add the powdered sugar gradually. Keep adding until a soft dough forms—it should be pliable, not sticky.

**4. Roll it out.** Lay out parchment paper and dust it with powdered sugar. Place the dough on top and dust the top lightly, too. Roll into a rectangle about ½-inch thick.

**5. Spread the peanut butter.** Spread the peanut butter evenly over the dough, leaving about a ½ inch border on one long edge.

**6. Roll it up.** Using the parchment to help you, roll it up tightly into a log. This is the part where you may whisper words not fit for a church bulletin. That's normal.

**7. Chill.** Wrap the log in plastic wrap and refrigerate 3 hours (or freeze for about 1 hour).

**8. Slice and serve.** Slice into pinwheels and serve. Try not to eat the end pieces "just to test it" five times.

## Kitchen Tips

* Start with 5 cups powdered sugar, then add more as needed. Potatoes vary, and this candy is moody like that.
* If you find that the dough is too sticky to work with, dust it with more powdered sugar.
* If the peanut butter is too stiff to spread, microwave it for 5 to 10 seconds to loosen it up.
* Make Ahead: Roll the log and keep it wrapped in the fridge up to 3 days before slicing.
* Storage: Refrigerate the slices in an airtight container for up to 1 week.
* Freeze: Wrap the whole log tightly and freeze up to 2 months. Thaw slightly before slicing.

# The House That Built Me

Junior year of high school—old enough to understand what was happening, young enough to feel like it was somehow my job to fix it.

My parents were on the cusp of finalizing their separation. They'd been living in that in-between space since I was in middle school, where everything is technically "fine," but you can feel the fracture in the air like humidity before a storm. And then, right as I was finishing high school, they finally decided to cut the cord.

I'm an only child, which means that I was trying to single-handedly hold a whole family unit together with zero support from any side. Do not recommend.

It's exhausting. It's confusing. It's emotionally loud. And it gives you the kind of hyper-awareness that makes you read a room the way some people read subtitles.

Now, let me say this: I love my parents dearly. They did what they believed was best at the time. This is not a chapter about bitterness. This is just a part of my story. A tender part. A forming part. But in that season, I wanted one thing more than anything: I wanted us together.

Every day, I'd go pick up my best friends and drive us to school. We carpooled. It was routine—drive, laugh, talk, pretend everything was normal, go be a teenager. On the way to their house, I'd pass this little side street.

And every now and then, I'd turn down that street. I wasn't lost. I wasn't running late and trying to take a shortcut. I just felt pulled. And one day, I noticed a house. It was being remodeled. New boards, fresh paint. And I thought, *What a cute little house.*

It was the kind of house you'd put a family in, where you'd hang stockings and hear laughter from the kitchen and feel safe when you walked in the door.

I started dreaming about it—because that's what kids do when they're trying to survive something too big. They create a picture, a plan, a "maybe if."

And somewhere in those drives, I began to pray a very specific prayer: *Lord, please let my mom and dad get back together. Please let us live together in that house.* I could see it. I could feel it. I could almost taste the stability of it. And then, I graduated. Life moved forward, whether my heart was ready or not. I didn't have to pick up my friends anymore, so I didn't drive by that street anymore. I didn't think about that house.

I tucked the dream away like an old picture in a drawer—still there, but not in my hands every day. And I moved on. Then, a couple years later, I met a boy. Tall, dark, handsome, and he felt like the kind of safe that doesn't have to announce itself. He made me feel steady in a way I didn't even realize I was craving.

We knew pretty quickly we were in it for the long haul. And one winter night, he said, "Hey, I've got to go turn on the water at the rental units in town. Do you want to ride with me?"

Now, let me explain something to the non-Floridians: When it freezes in Florida, we don't know how to act. We're not built for it. Our pipes aren't built for it. Our plants aren't built for it. We let pipes drip because if we don't, the water freezes, and the pipes burst, and then you have a real expensive problem on your hands.

So, he drives us around town turning on water and dripping pipes, and eventually, we turn down a street . . . and into a driveway.

And my whole body recognizes it before my brain does. I look out the window and I say, "Wait . . . I know this house."

And I'm staring at it like I'm looking at a ghost of my own past. "I used to drive by this house every day in high school," I explain. "And I used . . . to dream about having a perfect family in this house."

And he says, so casually, "Well . . . my dad and I remodeled this house and put it on the market. But in 2008, the market crashed, nobody wanted it, and nobody has lived in it. We remodeled it, and it's been empty ever since."

And I just . . . blinked. Because what do you do with that? What do you do when the house you prayed over as a teenager—back when your heart was breaking—turns out to be tied to the man sitting beside you?

It felt too strange to be random. It felt like God was quietly peeking through the curtain like, "Hey. Watch this." We left. Months went by. He proposed. A year went by. We got married. We were living in an apartment, and one night, he came home and said, "Hey . . . do you want to move into that house?"

And I said, "Yes!" It was a yes that sounded like a door opening in my soul.

We moved in fast—like when you're young and newly married and everything feels like an adventure.

Overnight, we packed up our apartment, hauled our stuff over, and stepped into that little house like it had been waiting for US.

And y'all . . . we lived in it. We didn't just exist there. We *lived*. We brought babies home to that house. We hosted showers and parties and milestones. We laughed in the kitchen, cried in the staircase, prayed in that bedroom, celebrated in the dining room.

We built a life—a real one. Not perfect like my teenage self imagined—because grown-up life is not a Pinterest board. But it was perfect in a deeper way. Perfect like: *safe*. Perfect like: *steady*. Perfect like: *we're here, we're together, and we're loved.*

And I didn't realize until later how much that house was healing parts of me I didn't even know were wounded. Because sometimes, God doesn't answer your prayers by rewinding the story. Sometimes, He answers by redeeming it. 10 years passed in what felt like a blink.

And then the day came: We were moving out of that home into our forever home, the one we'd been building. It was the one we prayed over and planned and poured ourselves into, the one that was closer to the family farm. And as excited as I was, I felt . . . uneasy. Because packing up a decade's worth of memories will do that to you.

One morning, I was putting things into boxes, wrapping up pieces of our life in paper and tape, when I heard it. Not out loud like someone in the room. But that unmistakable voice in your spirit. Just three words: "Do you remember?" And I froze. Because I did.

I flashed back to that 16-year-old girl driving down a side street, longing for a kind of wholeness she couldn't manufacture. I remembered looking at that house and praying: *Let me have a perfect family in this house.*

And in that moment, standing there with boxes at my feet, I realized something so tender it made my chest ache:

Not only was my prayer answered . . . it was answered in a way I never could've imagined. Because God didn't bring my parents back together. He didn't answer my prayer in the small, specific way I thought I needed. But He gave me a home where I got to build a family that stayed. He gave me a love that felt safe. He gave me children who would run through those rooms with joy. He gave me a decade of healing hidden inside ordinary days—inside family dinners and laundry and Christmas mornings and spilled cups and bedtime prayers.

It was like Heaven leaned close and whispered: "Hey. I didn't forget you." And y'all . . . I cried. Not the cute one-tear kind. The ugly gratitude kind. The kind where you can't even talk because your throat is tight and your heart is overflowing and you're realizing you were held all along.

So, I guess I'm telling you this because I don't know what your prayer is. I don't know what you've been asking for. I don't know what you've been carrying. I don't know what you whisper to God late at night when nobody else can hear. But I do know this: Sometimes, it feels like heaven is silent when you're begging for an answer. Sometimes, it feels like God has turned a deaf ear.

But what if . . . He hasn't? What if He's just not answering it in the limited way you can currently imagine? What if the story He's writing is bigger than the one you're trying to hold on to? Because I've learned—sometimes painfully, sometimes beautifully—that God's "not yet" is not a "no."

It's often mercy, often redemption, often Him building something grander than what you could've ever planned. So, do I know what tomorrow brings? No, I don't.

But I know who holds tomorrow. And I know He is kind enough to bless us in ways we can't comprehend—sometimes quietly, sometimes slowly, sometimes over the course of 10 ordinary years in a house you almost forgot.

And if you're in a season where you're waiting—where it feels like nothing is changing—where you're tempted to think you've been overlooked . . . Just hear me: You haven't. You are not forgotten.

And one day, you might be packing up boxes in a kitchen you love, and hear the gentlest voice say, "Do you remember?"

And you'll realize the whole time . . .

He was answering you. Even then. Even there. Even when you couldn't see it.

# Mawmaw Cake

## *(a.k.a. Call It What You Want, It's Still Mawmaw Cake)*

**SERVES 16**

**prep:** 10 minutes | **cook:** 40 to 45 minutes | **total:** 55 minutes *(plus cooling time)*

*Some of y'all may call this chess cake. Some of y'all may call it ooey-gooey butter cake. But in my family? This is Mawmaw Cake. It has been Mawmaw Cake my entire life, and I will not be taking questions at this time. It's the kind of dessert that doesn't require a special occasion—because it becomes the occasion.*

**Softened butter, for greasing the baking dish (don't be shy)**

**CRUST**

- **1 (15.25-ounce) box classic yellow cake mix**
- **1 large egg**
- **½ cup (1 stick) salted butter, melted**

**GOOEY LAYER**

- **8 ounces cream cheese, softened**
- **½ cup (1 stick) salted butter, melted**
- **2 large eggs**
- **4 cups powdered sugar**
- **1 to 2 teaspoons vanilla extract**

**MAKE THE CRUST**

**1. Preheat and prep.** Preheat your oven to 350°. Grease a 13x9-inch baking dish generously with butter. If you think it's too much butter, you're new here.

**2. Make the crust.** In a bowl, mix together the cake mix, egg, and melted butter until a thick dough forms. Press it evenly into the bottom of your greased dish.

**MAKE THE GOOEY LAYER**

**1. Make the gooey layer.** In a separate bowl, beat the cream cheese, melted butter, and 2 eggs with a mixer at medium speed until smooth. Add the powdered sugar gradually (unless you enjoy living in a powdered-sugar snow globe). Stir in the vanilla.

**2. Assemble.** Pour the filling over the crust and spread it out evenly.

**3. Bake the cake.** Bake for 40 to 45 minutes, until the edges are set and lightly golden, and the center is still a little jiggly. Do not overbake. The jiggle is the magic.

**4. Cool and slice.** Let cool at least 30 minutes before slicing. (Or don't. Just know it'll be lava, and you'll deserve it.)

# Mississippi Mud Cake

**SERVES 16**

**prep:** 20 minutes | **cook:** 30 to 35 minutes | **total:** About 1 hour *(plus cooling)*

*Mississippi Mud Cake isn't here to be cute. It's here to comfort you. It's chocolate cake, marshmallow fluff, and warm cocoa icing poured on top like a blanket you can eat. This is the kind of dessert my Mawmaw made when she wanted everybody to hush and just enjoy something good. It's messy, rich, and unapologetic.*

**Softened butter (for greasing the baking dish)**

CAKE

- 2 **cups granulated sugar**
- 2 **cups all-purpose flour**
- ½ **teaspoon salt**
- 1 **cup (2 sticks) salted butter**
- ⅓ **cup unsweetened cocoa powder (Hershey's is classic here)**
- 1 **cup water (or hot coffee, if you want it extra rich)**
- ½ **cup whole buttermilk**
- 2 **large eggs**
- 1 **teaspoon vanilla extract**
- 1 **teaspoon baking soda**
- 1 **cup chopped pecans (optional)**
- 1 **(7-ounce) jar marshmallow creme/fluff**

COCA-COLA CHOCOLATE ICING

- ½ **cup (1 stick) salted butter**
- ¼ **cup unsweetened cocoa powder**
- ¼ **cup Coca-Cola**
- ¼ **cup whole milk (or swap for more Coca-Cola)**
- 3½ **to 4 cups powdered sugar**
- 1 **teaspoon vanilla extract**
- **Pinch of salt**

BAKE THE CAKE

**1. Preheat and prep.** Preheat oven to 350°. Grease 13x9-inch baking dish with butter.

**2. Make the cake batter.** In a large bowl, whisk together sugar, flour, and salt. In a medium saucepan over medium heat, melt butter; whisk in cocoa powder until smooth. Pour in water (or coffee) and bring to a gentle boil; remove from heat. Pour cocoa mixture into dry ingredients; stir until combined. In a separate bowl, whisk together buttermilk, eggs, vanilla, and baking soda. Stir into the batter. Fold in pecans, if using. Pour into prepared dish.

**3. Bake it.** Bake until a toothpick inserted in the center comes out with a few moist crumbs, 30 to 35 minutes.

**4. Fluff it.** As soon as the cake comes out of the oven, spread marshmallow fluff over the top.

MAKE THE ICING

**1. Make Coca-Cola Chocolate Icing.** In a saucepan, melt butter. Whisk in the cocoa powder until smooth. Add the Coca-Cola and milk, and bring to a simmer over medium; remove from heat. Whisk in powdered sugar, vanilla, and salt until glossy and pourable. If it's too thick, add a teaspoon more milk or Coca-Cola. If it's too thin, add a little more powdered sugar.

**2. Pour and set.** Pour the warm icing over the fluff layer. Let the cake cool and set before slicing (if you can stand it).

# Steaks and A Chocolate Cake

We have around 12 seasons in the great state of Florida. And before anybody from up North tries to correct me—sweetheart, I'm not asking. This is lived experience. We have about a week of winter, fake spring, second winter, the pollening (which is not a season, it's a spiritual attack), actual spring, lovebug season (a flying insect with the personality of a clingy ex), summer, the devil's front porch, hurricane season, fake fall, second summer, and then—if the Lord is willing and the humidity takes a nap—actual fall.

Some of these seasons last for mere days, while others stretch on for months. And sometimes, it feels like the worst seasons get the longest time frames.

Every year, starting June 1, we Floridians participate in a little tradition called Hurricane Season, which runs from June through November. Tourists get nervous about it, and I understand. If you didn't grow up with the yearly possibility of your patio furniture relocating to another county, that's a lot to process.

But for the rest of us? It's just . . . life. While the rest of the country watches The Weather Channel, packs evacuation bags, buys batteries and water, watches The Weather Channel some more, prepares the generator, boards up the house, and panic-refreshes the radar like it's a hobby . . . Floridians are buying snacks and alcohol and praying the hurricane hits on a schoolday or workday.

We plan hurricane parties. We make jokes about the hurricane's name. We stand in the front yard like we're auditioning for a documentary called *I Should Not Be Outside Right Now*. And we do not freak out until a very specific meteorologist shows up. Because when that guy arrives, it's no longer "a little weather." It's a plot twist.

If you don't know who this specific meteorologist is, then bless you—you've never had to look at a man on television and think, Well . . . *I guess we're about to meet the Lord*. Some hurricane seasons are more active than others, and it's always a toss up whether the current season is going to produce a real monster, or just a bunch of named rainstorms that inconvenience your hair.

Now, if you're reading this and thinking, *What even is a hurricane?*—I'm not a meteorologist, and I don't pretend to be, but I can tell you what I know as a Florida native with a pantry full of batteries.

In tropical climates, the ocean water gets warm—real warm—during the summer and early fall. Warm, wet air rises, cooler air moves in to replace it, the cycle repeats, and storm clouds start forming. Add the rotation of the earth and a little atmospheric drama, and you've got yourself a system that can grow into a tropical depression, then a tropical storm (when it gets a name), and then a hurricane when the winds hit 74 mph or higher.

And here's the wildest part: Hurricanes have an eye. An actual calm center. The storm is roaring all around it—the wind, the rain, the noise, the destruction—but the eye is quiet. Blue sky sometimes. Stillness.

A moment to breathe before the eyewall hits again.

That concept used to fascinate me as a kid, because it felt like a metaphor even before I had enough life experience to know it was.

And for most of my life, hurricanes were exactly that—metaphors. Mild inconveniences. A reason to stay home. An excuse to make soup and light a candle and say dramatic things like, "Well, if the power goes out, we'll just eat all the ice cream first." I was raised in the kind of Florida where hurricanes were something you talked about more than something you feared.

In 2004, for instance, the Atlantic Ocean was acting like it had something to prove. I was in eighth grade, and from August to October, it felt like we were out of school every other week because a storm was "in the area." The school board would cancel classes out of an abundance of caution—which was wonderful for us, because half the time, we'd wake up to a perfectly sunny day and spend it like a bonus Saturday.

Florida got hit hard that year, and I never want to downplay what those storms did to people's homes and lives. But for a kid like me, hurricane season just felt like disruption, not devastation.

Then came July 2005—my first international trip. It was my first time flying, and I was going to Brazil with my Pawpaw, the man who had spent his life building churches and pouring himself out for other people. Our flight path was Tallahassee to Miami, then Miami to Manaus. And a few days before our departure, a tropical system formed and strengthened quickly—Hurricane Dennis.

We flew into Miami already feeling it: The outer bands. The restlessness. That heavy, churning sky that makes the air taste like metal and nerves.

I assumed—because I was young and had absolutely no idea what I was talking about—that our flight would be grounded. I thought we'd sit in Miami eating overpriced airport food until the storm passed. But apparently, Brazilian airlines are built on faith, courage, and the refusal to let weather ruin a schedule. The pilots assured us they would simply ascend and fly over the hurricane. "Simply." Like you do. So, we boarded.

Now listen—airplanes are not supposed to free-fall. That's not what they're for. That's not what anybody signed up for. Turbulence is one thing. This felt like the sky was playing hopscotch with the plane.

And I—being on my very first flight—was sitting mid-cabin, totally oblivious to how bad it actually was. I think I was laughing at the sensation, like, *Oh wow! It's like a roller coaster! Look at me living my best international life!*

Pawpaw, however, was sitting in the back of the cabin. He had taken hundreds of flights to Brazil. And when we landed in Manaus, my Pawpaw nearly kissed the ground. He told me later that while I was up there giggling like I was at Disney World, he was in the back praying for our survival.

In all his years of flying, he said that was the worst flight he had ever been on. And even then—after flying through the outer bands of a hurricane—my conclusion was still, *See? We're fine. Hurricanes are just dramatic rain.* That was my relationship with hurricane season: Casual. Light. A little sarcastic. Until October 2018. Until Hurricane Michael. If you didn't live through it, it's hard to explain how surreal the days before landfall felt. The skies were bright. The breeze was mild. It didn't match the fear on the forecast. It didn't match the tightening in your chest when you felt the pressure dropping and the storm strengthening.

It felt like standing in the calm part of a story right before the page turns. We prepared like Floridians do: water, nonperishables, batteries, medications, a plan. We weren't panicking—yet. The day before landfall, I went to the gym, and the mood in there felt . . . heavy. Everybody was talking, but nobody was saying anything comforting. There was that jittery energy in the air—like your body knows before your brain admits it.

I went home and thought, *Should I go to the grocery store? I don't need anything, but I feel like I do.*

So, I drove to our small-town grocery store at 6:45 a.m., and there was a line at the door. A line. In my little town.

It was one of the strangest things I'd ever seen—grown adults gathered like it was Black Friday, but instead of TVs, they were after canned goods and water. The moment the doors opened, people started running.

I didn't run. I just . . . walked in. Calmly. Almost too calmly. Looking back, I think I was disassociating. My body went into autopilot, like, we are not going to feel this right now. We are going to function.

People were snatching milk and bread off the shelves—which has never made sense to me, because if you think power is going out, why are you buying items that expire in 12 minutes?

Meanwhile, I was strolling through the aisles like I had all the time in the world thinking, *Steaks. We should have steaks. And a chocolate cake for dessert.* Somebody could've been yelling, "Ma'am, do you understand there's a Category Five storm headed our way?" and I would've been like, "Yes, but do y'all have cocoa powder?"

When I got to the register, the sweet clerk looked at my items like I had lost my mind. "This is it?" she asked. "You don't need anything else?" I answered, "No ma'am. I stocked up at the beginning of the season. I just needed dinner for tonight."

She blinked at me like, *This woman is making a cake while the world is ending.* And she wasn't wrong. When I got home, my husband told me we needed to go out to the farm—his parents' place about 20 miles away.

Farming families don't evacuate. They can't. When you're responsible for land and livestock and everything that comes with that kind of life, somebody has to stay. Somebody has to be the anchor.

My husband said the safest thing would be to go that night, not wait and travel in the outer bands the next morning. I didn't want to go. I wanted to stay in our house. That house wasn't just drywall and paint. It was the home I had prayed for when I was in high school. It was comfort. It was stability. It was proof that some of my dreams had come true.

I didn't want to abandon it. So, I told him I'd consider it, and then I did what I do when I'm anxious but pretending I'm not: I cooked.

I marinated the steaks like I was sealing in security. I made that chocolate cake like I could frost normalcy onto a storm.

When my husband got home, he was even more insistent. The pressure had dropped again, which meant the storm was strengthening. The tone in his voice was not "we should," it was "we must."

I reluctantly agreed—still thinking, in the back of my mind, that he might be overreacting. And I said, with full Southern sarcasm and zero prophetic awareness: "I'll go . . . but not without eating dinner first. If this is the last meal we have in this house, at least it'll be a good one." I said it like a joke. But wouldn't you know it . . . That was the last meal we had in that house for almost a year.

Hurricane Michael tore through our area as a devastating Category Five storm. We lost our home. A massive oak tree fell straight through the second story and obliterated the plumbing in the main bathroom. When the water came back on—because the city turned it off during the worst of the storm—it rained inside our house for nearly three days.

Not metaphorically. Literally. When the interstate finally reopened and we were able to go back home, we walked in the back door and found the ceiling on the floor. And the chocolate cake . . . was still right where I left it.

Sitting there like a little time capsule of who I was before the storm—still believing I could control the ending if I just kept stirring.

I stood in the wreckage and looked at that cake, and something in me broke in a quieter way than the hurricane had broken the house. Because grief is like that. It doesn't always arrive screaming.

Sometimes, it arrives as a still moment where your brain finally catches up to reality and your body says, *Oh. We are not okay.* I wish I could tell you I had a wise, poetic thought right then. Truthfully, I just stood there and tried to breathe. I thought about the eye of the hurricane—the calm that fools you into thinking the worst is over—when really, it's just a pause between waves. And that's what loss feels like sometimes.

There's the impact, and then there's the quiet after.

It's the strange stillness where you're walking around, making decisions, answering questions, doing what needs to be done, while your heart is trying to accept what happened.

I learned a lot in that storm. I learned that you can do everything "right" and still lose things you love.

I learned that home is not just a place—it's a feeling, and when that feeling gets ripped out from under you, you have to rebuild it slowly, from the inside out.

I learned that courage doesn't always look like confidence. Sometimes, it looks like showing up to a destroyed house and taking one more step anyway.

When life feels uncontrollable, we reach for what we can hold. And sometimes, in the middle of rubble, a chocolate cake is not just dessert. Sometimes, it's comfort. Sometimes, it's a memory. Sometimes, it's the last sweet thing you made before life got hard.

So today, I want to share that chocolate cake recipe—the one I made on that bright, breezy October day when nothing felt real yet. The one I baked while pretending I wasn't scared.

The one that sat in a broken house like proof that storms can take a lot . . . but they don't get to take everything.

Make it on a hard day. Make it on a good day. Make it when you're celebrating and make it when you're surviving.

And if you've ever found yourself standing in the aftermath of something you didn't see coming—honey, I hope this reminds you: There will be sweetness again.

Even if you have to start with one slice at a time.

## Kitchen Tips

- Room-temp eggs matter. They mix in smoother and help the cake bake evenly.
- Check your leaveners. Expired baking powder/soda will leave you with a sad, flat cake—and we don't do sadness in chocolate form.
- Don't overmix. Mix until combined, then stop. Overmixing makes the cake dense and dry.
- Parchment paper is awesome. It helps the cake bake evenly and release cleanly.
- Maintain medium heat for making the frosting. High heat can scorch the chocolate and make the frosting grainy. Gentle and patient wins the race.
- Make Ahead: Cake layers can be baked 1 day ahead. Wrap tightly and store at room temp.
- Frosting can be made up to 3 days ahead and stored in the fridge. Let it sit at room temp and stir until spreadable.

# Classic Chocolate Cake

## *(a.k.a. The Cake That Withstood the Hurricane)*

SERVES 10 TO 12

**prep:** 25 minutes | **cook:** 25 to 30 minutes | **total:** 3 hours *(includes cooling + frosting chilling)*

*This is my go-to chocolate cake when I need something rich, tender, and dramatic. The secret is the hot coffee. It doesn't make the cake taste like a latte; it just wakes up the cocoa and makes it deeper, darker, and just . . . better. The frosting? It's basically a chocolate truffle. Thick, glossy, and perfectly fudgy.*

Softened butter (for greasing the parchment paper)

CAKE

- 2½ cups all-purpose flour
- 1½ cups granulated sugar
- 2 teaspoons baking powder
- 1 teaspoon baking soda
- ½ teaspoon salt
- ½ cup unsweetened cocoa powder
- ⅔ cup whole buttermilk
- ⅔ cup vegetable oil
- 1 teaspoon vanilla extract
- 3 large eggs, room temperature
- 1 cup hot coffee (strong—espresso or instant coffee works, too)

CHOCOLATE FUDGE FROSTING

- 1½ cups (3 sticks) salted butter
- 14 ounces good-quality dark chocolate, chopped
- 1 cup heavy cream
- ⅓ cup unsweetened cocoa powder
- 1½ cups powdered sugar
- ½ teaspoon salt
- 1 teaspoon vanilla extract

Flaky salt for razzle dazzle (optional)

BAKE THE CAKE

**1. Preheat and prep.** Preheat your oven to 350°. Line two 8-inch round cake pans with parchment paper and lightly grease the sides with butter.

**2. Mix the dry ingredients.** In a large bowl, whisk together the flour, sugar, baking powder, baking soda, and salt. Sift in the cocoa powder and whisk again until evenly combined.

**3. Add the wet ingredients (except coffee).** Add the buttermilk, vegetable oil, vanilla, and eggs. Whisk until almost combined.

**4. Add the hot coffee.** Pour in the hot coffee and whisk just until smooth and no flour streaks remain. The batter will be runny—that's not a mistake, that's the magic.

**5. Bake.** Divide the batter evenly between the two pans. Bake 25 to 30 minutes, or until a toothpick inserted in the center comes out clean (a few moist crumbs are fine).

**6. Cool completely.** Let the cakes cool in the pans for 10 to 15 minutes, then turn out onto a rack to cool fully before frosting.

MAKE THE CHOCOLATE FUDGE FROSTING

**1. Melt it down gently.** In a saucepan over medium to medium-low heat, add the butter, chopped dark chocolate, and heavy cream. Stir constantly until melted and smooth.

**2. Add the powders.** Sift in the cocoa powder and powdered sugar; add the salt and stir until silky. Remove from heat and stir in the vanilla.

**3. Chill to thicken.** Transfer the frosting to a bowl and refrigerate 1 to 2 hours, stirring every so often, until it's thick, spreadable, and no longer warm.

ASSEMBLE

**1. Layer and frost.** Dot your cake stand with frosting so the cake doesn't slide. Place one cake layer on that dot of frosting. Spread a generous layer of frosting on top. Add the second layer and frost the top and sides.

**2. Optional razzle dazzle.** Sprinkle a little flaky salt over the top right before serving. It makes the chocolate sing.

# My Favorite Pound Cake

SERVES 12 TO 14

**prep:** 15 minutes | **cook:** 1 hour to 1 hour 10 minutes | **total:** 1 hour 40 minutes

*She's buttery and dressed up with just a whisper of rum extract—nothing that'll scandalize your Mamaw, but enough to make folks ask, "What is that flavor?" The real star, though? The butter-and-sugar Bundt pan. The crust comes out with a sweet little crunch every time.*

---

Softened butter (for greasing the pan)
2 to 3 tablespoons granulated sugar (for "sugaring" the pan)

CAKE

1 cup (2 sticks) salted butter, room temperature
3 cups granulated sugar
4 large eggs, room temperature
1 teaspoon vanilla extract
½ teaspoon rum extract
3 cups all-purpose flour
1 teaspoon baking powder
¼ teaspoon salt
½ cup whole milk
¾ cup sour cream

BROWN BUTTER GLAZE

½ cup (1 stick) unsalted butter
2 cups powdered sugar (sifted if you're feeling fancy)
1 teaspoon vanilla extract
Pinch of salt
3 to 5 tablespoons whole milk (or heavy cream if you're living your best life)

---

BAKE THE CAKE

**1. Prep the oven and pan.** Preheat your oven to 325°. Generously grease a 10-cup Bundt pan get butter in every crease like you're painting a masterpiece. Add 2 to 3 tablespoons sugar to the pan; rotate/tap until the inside is coated. This is how you get that sweet, crackly crust that makes people close their eyes when they chew.

**2. Cream butter and sugar.** In the bowl of a stand mixer, cream the butter and 3 cups sugar, beating with a mixer on medium speed until light and fluffy, about 3 to 4 minutes.

**3. Add the eggs and extracts.** Add the eggs one at a time, mixing just until combined after each. Mix in the vanilla and rum extracts.

**4. Mix the dry ingredients.** In a separate bowl, whisk together the flour, baking powder, and salt.

**5. Alternate additions (the process matters, so don't fight it).** Add half of the dry mixture to the batter and mix on low speed until just combined. Add the milk and sour cream and mix gently until incorporated. Add the remaining dry mixture and mix just until combined. Do not overmix. Pound cake is sturdy, but we're not trying to build a retaining wall.

**6. Bake and cool.** Pour batter into prepared Bundt pan and smooth the top. Bake until a toothpick inserted comes out clean (or with a few moist crumbs), 1 hour to 1 hour and 10 minutes. Let cool in the pan for 10 to 15 minutes, then invert onto a wire rack to cool completely.

MAKE THE BROWN BUTTER GLAZE

**1. Brown the butter.** Melt the butter in a light-colored saucepan over medium heat. Keep stirring as it foams and then starts to turn golden with little brown specks at the bottom. When it smells nutty, pull it off the heat.

**2. Cool slightly.** Let it sit for 5 minutes so it doesn't melt your powdered sugar into weird icing soup.

**3. Whisk the glaze.** In a bowl, whisk together the powdered sugar, vanilla, salt, and 3 tablespoons milk/cream. Slowly drizzle in the browned butter (include those brown bits—that's the flavor money). Add more milk/cream a splash at a time until it's pourable.

**4. Glaze the cake.** Drizzle glaze over cooled pound cake. Let it set for about 10 to 15 minutes before slicing . . . or don't. I'm not your boss.

## Kitchen Tips

- Glaze too thick? Add milk 1 teaspoon at a time. Too thin? Add a little more powdered sugar.
- Want to be extra? Sprinkle flaky salt on top while the glaze is still wet. It'll make the sweetness sing.
- Butter + sugar the pan is non-negotiable: It's the difference between "good cake" and "Why is this so addicting?"
- Room temp eggs help: smoother batter, better rise, fewer surprises.
- Don't rush the cool-down: If you flip it too soon, it can stick or crack. Patience is part of the recipe (unfortunately).
- Want to dress it up? Fresh berries and whipped cream make it company-ready in five seconds flat.
- Make Ahead: Bake 1 to 2 days ahead—this cake actually gets even better after it rests.
- Storage: Wrap tightly and keep at room temp for 3 to 4 days. OR Refrigerate up to 1 week, but bring to room temp before serving for best texture.

# 2

# Cornbread Stitches & Icon Wishes

This chapter is where things start getting unpredictable—which, frankly, is also very on-brand for me. Tucked between ridiculous moments, though, are the deeper things: faith, survival, wonder, and the understanding that life can change in an instant. It's also about food that feels humble but holds power. The kind of food that belongs to everyday people and ordinary kitchens.

# Cornbread Stitches & Icon Wishes

Life as a content creator (with cooking as one of my 51,214 niches) is a strange and wonderful dance.

You spend hours in your kitchen like a solo performer in an apron—talking to a ring light like it's your coworker, narrating your own decisions, and sending recipes out into the digital ether hoping they land. Most days, you're just you . . . in your kitchen . . . doing your best.

And then, one sun-drenched afternoon, I was deep in my element—not for the camera, but for a friend's party.

The kitchen was a controlled chaos. The sweet smell of butter and sugar danced through the air, that unmistakable, soul-soothing aroma of one of Mawmaw's cakes in the oven—the kind of cake that makes you feel like your childhood just walked through the door and said, "Sit down, honey. You've been through enough."

I was in the zone. Humming along with my Spotify. Blissfully unaware that the Internet was about to reach into my real life and grab me by the shoulders.

My phone vibrated.

It was a text from my childhood friend, Amber.

"Hey Meg, have you checked your social media today?"

Now, in my mind, this was the classic setup for something harmless, like a meme or a silly cat video. Something that would make me snort-laugh while I stirred.

So, I texted back, "No. I've been in the kitchen all afternoon. What's up?"

Her reply came back immediately. No greeting. No emoji. No "lol."

Just: "You're gonna wanna check your TikTok pretty quick." That was it.

And when a woman removes all pleasantries, you know you are either about to be celebrated . . . or publicly executed.

My stomach did a little flip. Even though you can't "hear" a tone through a text, I felt it in my bones. This wasn't giving "funny." This was giving "you are in danger."

My brain—trained in the fine art of catastrophizing—immediately began scrolling through a mental Rolodex of every possible online embarrassment.

Because if there is one thing I fear . . . it's a confident stranger with a comment section and time.

I wiped my hands on a dish towel, took a deep breath like I was about to open test results, and tapped the TikTok app.

The feed refreshed.

And there it was. A split screen.

My face next to Tim McGraw.

Not a man who looks like Tim McGraw.

Not a Tim McGraw impersonator from Missouri.

The actual, legendary, Grammy-winning, dimples-and-dreams Tim McGraw.

And he had stitched my fried cornbread video.

He wasn't just watching it—he was reacting to it.

Laughing. A real laugh.

His eyes crinkled. His shoulders bounced. He let out a genuine, hearty giggle at my jokes.

The man who sings heartbreaking ballads about lost love and dirt roads and emotional damage was chuckling at my commentary on cholesterol.

My brain did not compute.

I stared at the screen as if staring would suddenly make it make sense.

Because I could accept a lot of things, but Tim McGraw enjoying my fried cornbread content felt like a glitch in the simulation.

And that's when my nervous system hit the emergency eject button.

My phone left my hand.

It wasn't a throw so much as a full-body reflex—a convulsive launching. It arced through the air and landed with a soft thump into the couch pillows like it, too, needed a moment to process.

I stood there, mouth open, soul fully unzipped.

And then, I did what any respectable Southern woman does when confronted with something both thrilling and confusing:

I squealed. Not a cute little "oh my goodness."

A squeal. A sound that would make a dog tilt its head and a neighbor consider calling someone.

Because y'all . . . Tim McGraw. Tim. McGraw.

Of all the culinary mountains I've tried to climb for the camera—the elaborate cluster cakes, the multi-step recipes, the things that require 17 bowls and one emotional breakdown—it was the humble skillet of Fried Cornbread that did it.

A recipe woven into the fabric of my childhood.

A recipe that has been passed around like a family secret and served beside everything from field peas to fried chicken like it was the law.

It wasn't fancy. It wasn't trendy. It was just good.

And apparently, good is still good—even on the Internet.

In that moment, every hour of filming, every retake, every *does anyone even watch this?* thought, every time I edited a video while my food got cold . . . it all felt worth it.

Because I had been seen.

Not just by the social media algorithm.

By TIM MCGRAW.

And I know—fame is a funny thing. It's fleeting. It's weird. It's not the point of life. I get all that.

But I also believe God gives us little moments like that—sweet surprises that remind you you're not invisible. That the work you're doing matters. That the thing you thought was "too simple" might be the very thing that reaches somebody.

So yes, I stood there in my kitchen with cornbread on the stove and Tim McGraw on my phone and thought, *Well. This is what it feels like when the Lord sprinkles a little glitter on your Tuesday.*

Which is why it's only right that I share the recipe that started it all—my fried cornbread—along with a few of the other dishes I was curating when my friend sent that message and my nervous system left the chat.

Because in this world, you truly never know when you might whip up a little magic.

Sometimes, the thing that changes everything isn't the fanciest thing you make.

Sometimes, it's the simplest recipe. The kind that tastes like home. The kind that makes people laugh. The kind that makes you feel, for just a second, like you're exactly where you're supposed to be.

So . . . let's cook.

# Fried Cornbread
## *(a.k.a. The Skillet Magic That Made Tim McGraw Giggle)*

SERVES ABOUT 12

**prep:** 10 minutes | **cook:** 10 to 15 minutes | **total:** 20 to 25 minutes

*There are a million ways to make cornbread, but this one? This one is crispy, golden, and dangerously snackable—the kind of cornbread that doesn't even need a pot of beans to feel important. It's good with ham hocks, lima beans, mustard greens, collards . . . but it's also good standing alone at your kitchen counter at 11:17 p.m. with zero witnesses and absolutely no remorse.*

---

**1 cup medium-ground cornmeal (medium-sifted if you're fancy)**
**Sprinkle garlic powder**
**Sprinkle kosher salt**
**1 cup boiling water (has to be boiling to soften that cornmeal)**
**Peanut oil or vegetable oil, for frying (enough for about ¼-inch depth in skillet)**

---

1. **Make the dough (carefully, darling).** In a heat-safe bowl, whisk together the cornmeal, garlic powder, and salt. Pour the boiling water straight into the cornmeal mix, stirring immediately. Continue stirring until a thick dough forms. Let the dough cool until you can handle it safely. (It's hot. Don't be brave. Be alive.)
2. **Heat your oil.** Pour oil into a 9-inch skillet (cast iron is the love of my life here) to about ¼-inch deep. Heat over medium to medium-high heat until the oil looks like it has a little shimmer and movement. Test it: Drop in a tiny pinch of dough. If it bubbles right away, you're ready. If not, wait a few minutes and test again until it bubbles.
3. **Shape the cornbread rings.** Set out a sheet of parchment paper (or a plate) for your formed pieces. Scoop about 1 tablespoon of dough into your hand and pat it into a thin little round. If you love a crunch in every bite (I do), poke a small hole in the center like a cornbread donut. That hole helps the oil fry it evenly so you get crisp edges and a crispy center. Place formed rings on the parchment paper until you're ready to fry.
4. **Fry.** Carefully place a few rings into the hot oil; don't overcrowd them. Fry until golden, about 1 to 2 minutes. Flip gently and cook until golden, about 1 to 2 minutes. Transfer to a paper towel–lined plate to drain. Serve hot. Try not to eat six "taste tests" before supper. (You will.)

## Kitchen Tips

* Don't rush heating your grease. Too cool = greasy and sad. Too hot = burned outside, raw inside.
* Keep these thin—they fry faster, crispier, and more evenly.
* Peanut oil gives the best flavor and fry, but vegetable oil works just fine.
* Want to dress them up? Serve with honey, pepper jelly, or a swipe of butter while they're still warm.
* Make Ahead: Dough can be made a few hours ahead and kept covered at room temp until frying. (If it stiffens, add a tiny splash of warm water and mix.)
* Storage: Best fresh, but leftovers keep 2 days in an airtight container in the fridge.
* Reheat: Pop in a 350° oven for 8 to 10 minutes or an air fryer for a few minutes to bring back the crunch. Microwave will soften them . . . which is a personal choice, and I won't fight you, but I will sigh.

# Cornbread Cookies with Honey-Butter Frosting

**SERVES ABOUT 24** *(depending on how generous your scoop is)*

**prep:** 20 minutes | **cook:** 10 to 12 minutes | **total:** About 45 minutes *(includes cooling + frosting)*

*These taste like a warm skillet of cornbread and a bakery sugar cookie had a baby that grew up in the South with excellent manners and an addiction to honey-butter. They're soft, lightly gritty (in a good way), and sweet without being toothache-sweet—until you add the frosting, which is where the joy really lives. Finish them with honey and flaky salt and tell me you don't feel refreshed.*

CORNBREAD COOKIES

- ¾ cup granulated sugar
- ¾ cup firmly packed light brown sugar
- ½ cup salted butter, softened
- ½ cup shortening
- 2 large eggs
- 3 tablespoons honey
- 2 teaspoons vanilla extract
- 1 teaspoon baking powder
- 1 teaspoon kosher salt
- 1 cup cornmeal (medium or fine-ground—your choice)
- 3 cups all-purpose flour

HONEY-BUTTER FROSTING

- 3 cups powdered sugar
- 1 cup salted butter, softened
- 2 tablespoons honey
- 2 tablespoons heavy cream
- Pinch of kosher salt

RAZZLE DAZZLE
(optional but highly encouraged)

- Extra honey, for drizzling
- Flaky salt, for sprinkling

BAKE THE COOKIES

**1. Get the oven hot.** Preheat your oven to 350°. Line a few baking sheets with parchment paper.

**2. Make the dough.** In a stand mixer bowl, beat the granulated sugar, brown sugar, butter, and shortening on high speed until light and fluffy, about 3 to 5 minutes. Scrape the bowl. Turn mixer to low and add eggs, honey, vanilla, baking powder, and salt. Mix until combined. Scrape the bowl again. Mix in the cornmeal. Add the flour, one cup at a time, mixing just until smooth. The moment the dough comes together, stop mixing.

**3. Scoop the cookies.** Using a 3-tablespoon cookie scoop, scoop the dough; place the mounds 3 inches apart on the prepared baking sheets.

**4. Bake the cookies.** Bake for 10 to 12 minutes, until the centers are puffed and edges are lightly golden. Let the cookies cool on the baking sheets.

MAKE THE FROSTING

**1. Make it fluffy.** In a clean mixing bowl, beat all ingredients on low speed until mostly combined. Turn mixer to high and whip until smooth and fluffy.

FROST AND FINISH

**1. Decorate with the good stuff.** Pipe or spread the frosting onto the cooled cookies. Drizzle with a little extra honey.

**2. Add some razzle dazzle.** Sprinkle a tiny pinch of flaky salt on top if you like that sweet-salty magic.

## Kitchen Tips

- Cornmeal type matters: fine-ground gives a smoother cookie; medium-ground gives more "cornbread personality."
- Don't overbake: Remove them when the centers look set and the edges are barely golden. They'll stay soft.
- If the frosting feels thick: Add cream 1 teaspoon at a time until the frosting pipes/spreads easily.
- If the frosting feels loose: Add a little more powdered sugar and whip again.
- Make Ahead: Cookie dough can be scooped and chilled (covered) up to 48 hours. Bake straight from the fridge—add 1 minute if needed.
- Storage: Frosted cookies: Store in an airtight container in the fridge up to 5 days. Unfrosted cookies: Store in an airtight container at room temp 2 to 3 days.
- Serve: Bring to room temp for the best texture (and the best honey-butter vibes).

# A Blessing of The Sea

The sea has blessed people with many things over the course of human history. Pearls. Fish. Shipwrecked treasure. Ancient messages in bottles. And then . . . there's what it blessed me with. Ice cream. Not metaphorical ice cream. Not "the sweet treat of friendship" ice cream. I mean actual frozen, individually wrapped, king-sized ice cream bars—delivered via the Gulf like Neptune himself said, "She asked for dessert. Handle it."

And before you start thinking, *Meghan, that did not happen*, let me assure you: I have video evidence, and the eyewitness accounts of about 25 people who watched it unfold in real time. This was not a fever dream. This was a documented, ocean-certified blessing.

It started like any Florida birthday party: with good intentions, questionable weather, and the kind of optimism that borders on delusion.

A few years ago, we were invited to a child's birthday party on the beach—because nothing says "happy birthday" like sand in your chips and wind strong enough to snatch a paper plate straight into the afterlife.

On the drive to the party, the sky started doing that Florida thing where it looks perfectly fine . . . until it doesn't. The clouds gathered. The air got weird. The atmosphere began to swirl and take on the characteristics of a new personality. Now, Floridians know this rule: If you don't like the weather, wait 15 minutes; it'll change. Unfortunately, sometimes, it changes into a full-blown situation.

We arrived to the beach, and we began the long pilgrimage across the sand. And listen—walking in sand should count as cardio, CrossFit, and kickboxing. Because when you're walking through sand, 20 feet feels like two miles, and by the time you reach your destination, you've questioned every decision you've ever made since birth.

We finally reached the party tent, and right on cue, the sky opened up like it had been waiting for us to get settled. The bottom fell out. Rain came sideways. Lightning started popping off like paparazzi. The wind kicked up in a way that made the tent look less like a shelter and more like an aggressive kite trying to tour the world.

And here's the thing about me: I had just walked what felt like five miles to get to that tent. I was not turning around. I didn't care if the sand swallowed me whole. I didn't care if my hair turned into a salted tumbleweed. I looked the storm dead in its watery face and thought: *I'm already here. We'll work it out.* So, there were about 15 of us huddled under the tent—clinging to the poles, gripping the tent legs, holding on like we were auditioning for a beach-themed episode of the CBS reality show *Survivor.*

The rest of the people on the beach cleared out immediately. Most people possess something called "common sense." But do you know what Florida people are afraid of? Nothing. We don't evacuate. We don't scatter. We don't learn lessons. We just stand there and say, "WELL! This is unfortunate," like the sky didn't just throw hands with us.

And right in the middle of this tropical tantrum, I did what any responsible adult would do.

I turned to my friend and said, completely serious, "Hey . . . did you happen to bring ice cream to go with that birthday cake?"

She blinked at me like I had lost my mind—which I had, but that's beside the point.

"No," she said. And I nodded like a woman who understands disappointment and has endured it before.

"That's okay," I replied. "I'm just happy to be here."

Which is what you say when you're trying to be gracious but your spirit is privately grieving the lack of frozen dessert.

Well, the Gulf heard my heart.

As the storm began to clear, we looked toward the rocks at the end of the beach and noticed something that did not look right.

A boat . . . was on its side. And I'm not a marine expert, but I do know this: Boats are not supposed to do that.

So, we all watched as the people inside the boat climbed out and scrambled onto the rocks. They were shaken, but safe. And within two minutes, every boat within a mile radius came flying over like, "WE GOT YOU!" followed shortly by the Coast Guard—because Florida might be reckless, but we are also strangely efficient in emergencies.

For a brief moment, I thought, *Should we help?*

And then, I saw the Coast Guard.

And I was like . . . no. I think I'll stay in my lane. My lane is emotional support and maybe a casserole.

So, while the professionals handled the capsized boat, my attention drifted to something else in the water.

A big box. Floating. In the middle of the ocean. Just bobbing out there. And my first thought was: *Don't touch it.*

Because anytime a mysterious box washes up on the coast of Florida, there is a strong chance it contains something illegal, suspicious, or cursed.

My second thought was: *But what if it's interesting?*

So, naturally, I ignored my first thought.

I looked at my friends and said something along the lines of: "On today's episode of *Illicit Substances or Body Parts*, let's go see what the ocean has delivered."

And the closer I got to the box, the more my confusion grew because it *wasn't* a box.

It was a freezer. A literal 110-volt freezer. In the Gulf. Just out there, vibing. Now, you're probably wondering the same thing we were: *How. Why. What. Who.*

We waded out in the water and pulled the freezer toward the shore. It took two of us to carry it onto the sand. We got it stable and looked at each other, stunned. I turned to my friends and said, "Are y'all gonna open it?"

They said, "No. Are YOU gonna open it?"

And I'd like to tell you I hesitated. I'd like to tell you I weighed the risks. I'd like to tell you I called an adult.

But you and I both know that would be a lie. I opened it. And what I found inside . . . was ice cream.

Not a little bit. Not a sad, half-melted, questionable Popsicle situation. I mean filled to the brim.

King-sized ice cream bars. Giant frozen ice cream cones. Salted caramel chocolate ice cream bars. A treasure chest of frozen confections, delivered by Poseidon himself like: "Happy birthday. Love, the Sea." And the part that really took me out? The ice cream treats were still frozen.

Which means this freezer had been doing its job out there in the water long enough for it to become the world's most confusing blessing. I don't know how that's possible, and I don't care. I've made my peace with mysteries. Some things are meant to stay a mystery.

Now, I am going to say this for legal reasons and because I would like to stay out of trouble: The proper authorities were notified that there was a freezer on the beach. We are responsible citizens. We respect order. We love a procedure. And then . . . decisions were made.

Just know this: If you are wondering how many ice cream bars I can ingest in one sitting while adrenaline is still circulating through my bloodstream and the ocean has just personally provided dessert . . . The answer is five. Five.

I don't know who I was in that moment, but she was powerful, she was dairy-based, and she was living in the blessing. Because here's the thing: Sometimes, blessings look like a front-row parking spot. Sometimes, they look like a free coffee. Sometimes, they look like the right person calling at the right time. And sometimes . . .

They look like a freezer full of king-size ice cream bars washing up on the shore right after you casually asked for ice cream under a storm-whipped tent like a woman with audacity and a dream.

So, the next time life gets chaotic—when the wind is whipping, plans are ruined, and you're clinging to a metaphorical tent pole—remember this: You may not see it coming, but the blessing might already be floating your way. It might be joy. It might be peace. It might be something you didn't even know you needed. Or it might be an ice cream bar. Either way—don't be too proud to receive it.

In honor of the day the sea itself said, "Here, sis . . . have dessert," let's move into a recipe that tastes like celebration because sometimes the sweetest moments in life show up when everything feels like it's falling apart. And if you don't believe me? I've got 25 witnesses. And a video.

“Sweet(ish). Spicy. Dramatic. Finally, a recipe with my personality.”

*—Luci*

# Hot Honey Skillet Cornbread Cake with Buttermilk Ice Cream in a Bag

SERVES 8 *(or 6 if your family has no self-control)*

**prep:** 10 minutes | **cook:** 22 minutes | **total:** 32 minutes

*A good skillet cornbread will change your life, your standards, and possibly your personality. This version gets finished with a Hot Honey–Butter Drizzle that turns plain cornbread into a full-on event.*

CORNBREAD

- 2 tablespoons salted butter
- 1 cup yellow cornmeal
- 1 cup all-purpose flour
- 1 tablespoon baking powder
- 1 teaspoon kosher salt
- 1 cup whole buttermilk
- 2 large eggs
- ⅓ cup honey
- ⅓ cup vegetable oil

HOT HONEY—BUTTER DRIZZLE

- ½ cup (1 stick) salted butter, melted
- ¼ cup hot honey

ICE CREAM BASE

- ½ cup whole buttermilk
- ½ cup half-and-half
- 2 tablespoons granulated sugar
- Dash vanilla extract

THE ICE BATH

- Gallon-size Bag
- Ice, enough to fill the bag halfway
- Coarse salt

MAKE THE CORNBREAD

**1. Heat the skillet.** Preheat your oven to 400°. Add 2 tablespoons butter to a 9-inch cast-iron skillet and place it in the oven while it preheats.

**2. Mix the batter.** In a large bowl, whisk together the cornmeal, flour, baking powder, and salt. In a separate bowl, whisk together the buttermilk, eggs, honey, and oil. Pour the buttermilk mixture into the cornmeal mixture and whisk just until combined. Don't overmix, or you'll turn your cornbread into a brick with a nice personality.

**3. Bake.** Carefully remove the hot skillet from the oven. Swirl the melted butter around to coat the bottom and sides. Pour the batter into the skillet and bake until golden and set in the center, about 22 minutes.

**4. Drizzle like you mean it.** While the cornbread bakes, prepare the Hot Honey–Butter Drizzle. Whisk together the melted butter with the hot honey. As soon as the cornbread comes out, drizzle it generously over the top. Let it soak in for a few minutes, then slice and serve warm.

MAKE THE ICE CREAM

**1. Mix the base.** In a quart-size resealable plastic bag, add the buttermilk, half-and-half, sugar, and vanilla. Seal very well and shake a tad to combine.

**2. Build the ice bath.** Fill a gallon-size resealable plastic bag about halfway with ice. Add a generous pour of salt over the ice (think: a handful, not a whisper).

**3. Shake it like you mean it.** Place the sealed quart-size bag of ice cream inside the gallon-size bag of ice. Seal the gallon-size bag tightly. Shake for 10 minutes. (Yes, your arms will burn. That's the price of greatness.) It's ready when the mixture feels stiff and scoopable.

**4. Serve.** Wipe off the quart-size bag (nobody wants salty ice cream) and scoop ice cream onto a slice of cake drizzled with extra Hot Honey–Butter Drizzle, if desired.

## Kitchen Tip

* Wear gloves or wrap the ice cream bag in a towel unless you enjoy frostbite as a personality trait.

# Polly

Let me tell y'all why I don't speak to animals anymore. And before you ask—yes. This is a true story. Unfortunately for me, everything I'm about to say is 100% accurate. No embellishment. No "for the sake of storytelling." Just me, living out a plotline that should've been rejected in the writers' room.

So, we live in a residential neighborhood. From our front porch, you can see up the road a piece at one of those houses where the garage is downstairs, and there are two windows upstairs that stare right back at you like they know your business.

One day, a family moves into that house. I never saw moving trucks, but suddenly, there was . . . activity. Lights on. People coming and going. A life where there hadn't been one before. And after a few weeks, I noticed one of the upstairs bedroom windows was open.

Now listen. My family and I are porch people. We will sit on a porch swing like it's our full-time job. And one evening while we're out there, just swinging and minding our own business, we hear it: "Hello."

Like . . . bird hello. That little chirpy, breathy "Hello" that makes you picture a parrot in a golden cage, sipping out of a tiny water bottle and judging your outfit.

So naturally, we do what any responsible Southerner would do. We talk back. "Hello!" And sometimes, we'd get bold. "Polly want a cracker?"

Because those are the two approved phrases you're allowed to say to a talking bird. It's in the Constitution.

And y'all . . . for months . . . we had full-blown porch conversations with this "bird." Nothing deep. Just a friendly little back-and-forth. We'd say hello, and "Polly" would say hello. It was sweet. It was wholesome. It was like a Hallmark movie but with feathers.

And yes—I named the bird. Polly. Original? No. Effective? Absolutely.

Then, Hurricane Michael hits. A Category Five storm. Life-altering. We lost our house. We were displaced for almost a year while we rebuilt. And in the midst of all that trauma and debris and paperwork and insurance calls that make you question your salvation . . . do you want to know what I kept thinking about?

That bird. *Lord, I hope Polly is okay.* I was emotionally attached. I'm praying for the bird. I'm grieving the bird. I'm wondering if Polly has enough crackers.

We finally get back home months later. First week back, we step out on the porch . . . look up at that house . . . Window's open. And I hear it. "Hello." Y'all. I almost cried.

POLLY LIVED.

My feathered friend made it through the storm. God is faithful. Miracles still happen. The bird is thriving. We're back to chatting like no time has passed. Two years go by. Two. Years.

I have invested over two years of my one wild and precious life speaking to this "bird." Never once did I see it. Never once did I question it. Because birds are in cages, Meghan. Birds can be in a room you can't see. Birds are mysterious. Birds are . . . private.

One morning, I'm getting the kids ready for school, and I hear Polly say something new. Not "Hello." Not "Cracker." Polly says—clear as day— "Help." *Excuse me?*

HELP? Now, I'm laughing but also . . . not laughing. Because who taught the bird to say help? Why is Polly sounding so crisp today? The audio quality is suddenly high definition. Polly has upgraded microphones.

And then, I hear it again. "Help. Help." Something is off. Polly sounds . . . human.

So, I do what any sane person would do. I walk around the front of my house so I can see into that upstairs window. And y'all. It was an elderly woman. Hands outside the window. One leg outside the window.

Like she was halfway between "fresh air" and "I'm fixing to make a break for it."

And as I'm watching her, she looks down the street—right in my direction—and says: "Help." And in that moment

. . . my whole life rearranged itself. I had not been speaking to a bird. I had been speaking to a human being. For over TWO. YEARS.

Suddenly every "hello" I ever hollered from that porch swing played back in my mind like a crime documentary. Over two years of porch-swing bonding, and the whole time I thought I was building rapport with a parrot.

Do you know what that does to your spirit? Because, now I'm replaying my life like a courtroom exhibit: Me, thinking I'm Snow White, when really, I'm just confusing an elderly neighbor.

And even worse—I had been out there hooting and hollering "POLLY WANT A CRACKER" at a grown woman. Lord. So, of course, I run up the hill. I'm trying to be calm but come on.

"Ma'am! Are you okay? Can I help you?" I ask.

She looks at me—dead serious—and says, "I need a lawyer." A *lawyer.*

I have spent over two years saying hello and offering crackers. And now, we've escalated to legal counsel? I am not prepared for legal proceedings. But we got her help. We called the appropriate folks. We made sure she was safe. We did the right thing. And after that?

I never saw her again. Never heard her again. No more "Hello." No more "Help." No more porch swing friendship.

Just silence . . . and the lingering memory of me being emotionally invested in what I thought was a macaw but was actually a grandma.

So, here's the moral of the story: If you're going to talk to your pets . . . make sure you can see them. Because you might not be talking to an animal. You might be talking to a human going through it.

Because some birds don't lay eggs. And speaking of eggs: Here are my deviled egg recipes.

“Deviled Eggs?
That’s some branding
I can get behind.”

*—Luci*

# California Roll Deviled Eggs

SERVES 6 *(12 deviled egg halves)*

**prep:** 20 minutes | **cook:** 14 minutes
**total:** 34 minutes *(plus cooling)*

*Creamy yolk filling, a whisper of wasabi, and toppings that make people say, "Hold on . . . DEVILED EGGS can do that?" Yes, they can.*

THE EGGS

- 6 **large eggs**
- ¼ **cup mayonnaise**
- 1 **teaspoon wasabi paste**

THE TOPPINGS

- ½ **cup cooked crabmeat, picked over for shells**
- ⅓ **cup cucumber, thinly sliced or finely diced**
- ½ **avocado, thinly sliced or diced**
- **Yum yum sauce, for drizzling**
- **Black sesame seeds, for sprinkling**

BOIL THE EGGS *(no drama method)*

**1. Boil the eggs.** Bring a large pot of water and salt to a boil. Carefully lower in eggs and boil for 2 minutes. Turn the heat off, cover the pot, and let the eggs sit in the hot water for 12 minutes. (14 minutes total.)

**2. Cool and peel.** Transfer the eggs to an ice bath to cool completely. Peel only when fully cooled.

ALL ABOUT THE FILLING

**1. Halve and scoop.** Slice eggs in half lengthwise. Carefully scoop yolks into a bowl and set the whites on a platter.

**2. Make the filling.** Mash yolks with mayonnaise and wasabi until smooth and creamy. No lumps. We are not making egg gravel today.

**3. Pipe it pretty.** Spoon or pipe the filling into each egg white.

**4. Top like a sushi chef.** Add a little crab, then a bit of cucumber, and a slice of avocado.

**5. Finish the masterpiece.** Drizzle with yum yum sauce and sprinkle with black sesame seeds.

# Fried Deviled Eggs

SERVES 6 *(12 deviled egg halves)*

**prep:** 25 minutes | **cook:** 18 minutes
**total:** 45 minutes *(includes cooling)*

*Crispy on the outside, creamy in the middle, and just fancy enough to make people think you worked harder than you did.*

THE EGGS

- 6 **large eggs, hard-boiled and peeled**
- ¼ **cup mayonnaise**
- 1 **teaspoon smoked paprika, plus more for garnish**
- 1 **teaspoon sweet relish**
- 1 **teaspoon Dijon mustard**
- ½ **teaspoon Worcestershire sauce (say it however your heart leads you)**
- **Salt and ground black pepper, to taste**

THE FRYING ASSEMBLY LINE

- **Neutral frying oil**
- ½ **cup all-purpose flour**
- 2 **large eggs, beaten (for egg wash)**
- 1 **cup plain breadcrumbs**

MAKE THE FILLING

**1. Halve and scoop.** Slice eggs in half lengthwise. Carefully scoop yolks into a bowl and set the whites aside.

**2. Make the filling.** Mash yolks with mayonnaise, smoked paprika, sweet relish, Dijon mustard, Worcestershire, salt, and pepper until smooth and creamy. If it's lumpy, keep going.

BREAD AND FRY THE WHITES

**1. Heat the oil.** Pour oil into a 12-inch cast-iron skillet to about ½-inch deep and heat over medium heat.

**2. Set up your assembly line.** To a plate, add flour. To another plate, add eggs. To another plate, add breadcrumbs.

**3. Dredge the eggs.** Working with one egg white half at a time, coat in flour and shake off excess. Dip in the eggs. Roll in breadcrumbs until fully coated. Repeat until all are coated.

**4. Fry the eggs.** Fry in batches until golden brown, about 2 minutes per side. Transfer to a paper towel–lined plate and let cool slightly.

FILL AND FINISH

**1. Pipe it pretty.** Spoon or pipe the filling into each egg white.

**2. Finish the masterpiece.** Sprinkle with a little extra smoked paprika. Serve warm-ish or at room temp and watch people lose their minds.

# Parmesan Truffle Deviled Eggs

**SERVES 6** ***(12 deviled egg halves)***

**prep:** 15 minutes | **total:** 15 minutes

*If deviled eggs could wear a cashmere sweater and carry a tiny designer bag, these would be the ones. They're rich, they're boujee, and they taste like you said "yes" to the fancy menu without looking at the prices.*

- **6 large eggs, hard-boiled and peeled**
- **3 tablespoons mayonnaise**
- **2 tablespoons freshly grated Parmesan cheese, plus more for garnish**
- **1 tablespoon truffle oil**
- **¼ teaspoon garlic powder**
- **Ground black pepper, to taste (a couple good cracklin's)**

**OPTIONAL GARNISH**

**Truffle salt (a pinch on top)**

**1. Halve the eggs.** Slice the eggs lengthwise and gently pop the yolks into a bowl. Set the whites on a platter like the little egg boats they are.

**2. Make the filling.** Mash the yolks with mayonnaise, Parmesan, truffle oil, garlic powder, and black pepper. Mix until smooth, creamy, and luxurious.

**3. Fill the whites.** Spoon or pipe the filling into each egg white. Pipe them if you want them to look like they have a skincare routine and a matching luggage set.

**4. Garnish like you mean it.** Finish with a little extra Parmesan, a pinch of truffle salt (if you've got it), or another cracklin' of black pepper. Serve immediately or chill until party time.

# Ramen Deviled Eggs

**SERVES 6** ***(12 deviled egg halves)***

**prep:** 20 minutes | **cook:** 10 minutes
**marinate:** 6 hours minimum
**total:** 6 hours 30 minutes *(plus cooling marinade)*

*This is what happens when my love for deviled eggs and my love for ramen-shop marinated eggs decide to get married and move in together. They're savory-sweet, a little mysterious, and they taste like you've got your life together—even if you're eating them in sweatpants at the kitchen counter. Fair warning: These eggs need a long soak. Minimum 6 hours. Overnight is even better. Patience tastes delicious.*

**MARINATED EGGS**

- **1½ cups water**
- **1 cup soy sauce**
- **1 cup mirin**
- **½ cup packed dark brown sugar**
- **4 cloves garlic, smashed**
- **2 to 3 whole star anise**
- **A few slices fresh ginger**
- **6 large eggs, hard-boiled and peeled**

**FILLING**

- **¼ cup mayonnaise**
- **1 teaspoon honey (plus a little extra if you're feeling it)**
- **Ground black pepper, to taste (a couple good cracklin's)**

**TOPPING**

- **Furikake, for sprinkling**
- **Chopped green onion, for sprinkling**

**1. Make the marinade.** In a saucepan over medium heat, combine the 1½ cups water, soy sauce, mirin, brown sugar, garlic, star anise, and ginger. Bring it to a gentle simmer and stir until the sugar dissolves. Let it simmer 2 to 3 minutes, then remove from heat. Important: Let the marinade cool completely. Hot marinade + eggs = overcooked rubbery eggs, and we will not be chewing bouncy balls today.

**2. Marinate the eggs.** Place the peeled eggs in a container or plastic resealable bag. Pour the cooled marinade over the eggs. Refrigerate at least 6 hours—overnight is best. When they're ready, the whites should be a gorgeous brown, like they've been on vacation.

**3. Make the filling.** Remove the eggs from the marinade and pat them dry. Slice in half lengthwise and pop yolks into a bowl. Add the mayonnaise, honey, and black pepper. Mash and mix until smooth and creamy.

**4. Fill and finish.** Spoon or pipe the filling into the marinated egg whites. Sprinkle with the furikake and chopped green onion. Serve immediately—or chill until you're ready to be the fanciest person at the function.

# Sautéed Shrimp & Fried Pickled Okra Deviled Eggs

**SERVES 6** *(12 deviled egg halves)*

**prep:** 25 minutes | **cook:** 10 to 15 minutes | **total:** 35 to 40 minutes

*If you've ever looked at a deviled egg and thought,* This is great, but it needs to do more, *welcome. This is a deviled egg that showed up to the party in a full outfit: creamy filling, buttery Old Bay shrimp, and fried pickled okra that crunches like it has something to prove. It's the whole kit and caboodle. It's a Southern seafood boil in one bite.*

EGGS

- 6 large eggs, hard-boiled and peeled
- ¼ cup mayonnaise
- 1 teaspoon Dijon mustard
- ½ teaspoon Old Bay seasoning

FRIED PICKLED OKRA

- Vegetable oil, for frying
- 1 cup cornmeal
- ½ cup all-purpose flour
- 1 teaspoon garlic powder
- Salt and ground black pepper, to taste
- Whole pickled okra (about 10 to 12 pods, depending on size)
- 1 large egg, beaten (for egg wash)

SAUTÉED SHRIMP

- 12 small shrimp, peeled and deveined
- Old Bay seasoning, to taste
- 2 tablespoons unsalted butter

Garnish: chopped fresh chives

MAKE THE FILLING

**1. Halve and scoop.** Slice eggs in half lengthwise. Carefully scoop yolks into a bowl and set the whites on a platter.

**2. Make the filling.** Mash yolks with mayonnaise, Dijon mustard, and Old Bay. Mix until real smooth—the kind of smooth that makes you want to dip a cracker in it. Spoon or pipe into the egg whites. Set aside.

FRY THE OKRA

**1. Heat the oil.** Pour oil into a 12-inch cast-iron skillet to about ½-inch deep and heat over medium heat.

**2. Set up your assembly line.** In a medium bowl, mix together the cornmeal, flour, garlic powder, salt, and pepper. Pat okra dry and add to a plate. To another plate, add beaten egg for egg wash.

**3. Test the oil.** Take a pinch of the cornmeal mixture and drop in the oil. If it sizzles, you're ready to fry.

**4. Fry the okra.** Working in batches, dip okra into egg wash and then cornmeal mixture, tapping off excess. Fry until golden brown, about 1 to 2 minutes per side, depending on size. Transfer to a paper towel–lined plate to drain. Repeat until all okra is fried.

COOK THE SHRIMP

**1. Sauté the shrimp.** Season shrimp with Old Bay. In a skillet over medium heat, melt butter and add shrimp in a single layer. Cook about 2 minutes per side, until pink and just cooked through. Set aside.

ASSEMBLE AND SERVE

**1. Assemble the whole situation.** Top each deviled egg with 1 shrimp and 1 piece of fried pickled okra (or a smaller okra pod if you can find one). Finish with chopped fresh chives. Serve immediately while the okra still has that crunch.

# The Appendix & Grits

So, on today's episode of "Things That I Could Not Make Up If I Wanted To," I've got a story for you that still makes my eye twitch when I think about it. Trigger warning: This story involves medical stuff, surgery, and the kind of plot twist that makes you stare at the wall afterward and whisper, "Well . . . okay then."

In 2017, my family was headed to Tallahassee, Florida, to celebrate my Pawpaw's birthday. That morning, my stomach started burning, but I had just started exercising again. So, I did what every optimistic woman does when her body starts sounding an alarm: *I blamed it on crunches.*

"Ah yes," I told myself. "This is just my abs waking up. This is health." That feeling lingered all day, though. Nothing unbearable—just . . . off. Like my insides were sending vague emails instead of clear instructions.

We loaded up and made the drive anyway. On the way there, we spotted a young girl on the side of the interstate with a flat tire. It was January, school was starting back, and she looked like a college student who had run out of luck and air pressure. So, I told my husband to pull over.

Now let me clarify: I talked to her and made her feel taken care of. My husband, Seth, changed the tire. That's the division of labor in our household. Emotional support is my ministry, and manual labor is his love language. So, there we were, chatting, while—unbeknownst to me—my appendix was preparing for its final, dramatic monologue.

We made it to Tallahassee. Pawpaw's birthday dinner was pulled pork and all the fixin's. Everybody was laughing, eating, celebrating . . . and I was getting more nauseated. I tried to push through because I'm stubborn and was raised to believe you can solve most problems with sweet tea and denial. But after cake, I said, "I love y'all. We gotta go."

Halfway between Tallahassee and home, I became intimately acquainted with the reality that my dinner did not plan to stay with me. *Something was very, very wrong.*

I called a dear friend of mine who was an ER nurse. He said, "Come in now," in the tone that tells you he is not being dramatic—he is being helpful. We got to the hospital around 10 p.m. I got a CT scan around midnight. Then, the doctor came in and said, "Your appendix is really bad."

And I was like, "Okay . . . so you're going to take it out?" He said—without blinking—"Not tonight. I need some sleep. I've been in surgeries all day. We'll do it first thing in the morning." Now, I had never had surgery before. This was my first rodeo. And when you're in pain, in a hospital gown, and someone with a medical degree tells you, "We'll handle it," you don't exactly whip out a clipboard and start negotiating.

So, I said, "Okay." They gave me pain meds. I tried to rest. My appendix tried to set a world record for drama. The next morning, the surgical team came to get me.

Now, I still had on makeup from the night before because let me tell you—when you're in that kind of pain, you are not standing at a sink washing your face. You are not doing a double cleanse. You are not toning. You are surviving. So, I was there with yesterday's mascara and a weak spirit, and they were still acting like I was ready for prom. The anesthesiologist leaned in, placed that mask over my face, and told me, "Just breathe."

And I will never forget the last thing I heard before the lights went out. One of the nurses looked at me with the sweetest expression and said—almost like she was talking to the other nurses, not knowing I could still hear her—"She's so sweet . . . look at her." Y'all. That got me. Even in my drugged-up, terrified state, my heart heard it. Now . . . while we're here and while I'm already being vulnerable, let me confess something that makes this whole moment even more ridiculous.

I love a good spray tan. There is just something about that golden glow that makes me feel like I have my life together—whether I do or not. I normally get a bottle of my favorite tanner and apply it myself. But that stuff is expensive, and I don't like to waste product. So, in the winter? I am not tanning my stomach and legs. Why? Because who needs to do that? Ain't nobody viewing this body with less than a sweater and jeans in January.

And before you say, "But you're from Florida"—baby, I dress for the season, not for the temperature. If the calendar says winter, I'm in a sweater. I don't care if it's 78 degrees and sunny. So, I'm telling you this to say . . . when that doctor pulled the sheet back, he was in for a surprise. Because my body was only half spray-tanned. From the waist up, I was glowing like a bronzed angel. From the waist down, I was giving . . . Victorian ghost.

He probably thought I had bigger issues than a rupturing appendix. But I digress. Now, the surgical team had told my family: "Forty-five minutes to an hour tops. Very simple procedure. We'll bring her right back." Forty-five minutes. I want you to hold onto that number. Because an hour went by. Two hours. Three hours.

And by that point, my family was out there in the waiting room losing their minds, because hello, someone told them I was going to be back before breakfast, and now, it's creeping toward lunch.

Turns out my "quick little surgery" took almost five hours. When I finally woke up, I was convinced it was still the morning. I got back to my hospital room and was like, "Y'all . . . why does it feel like I've been asleep for five minutes?" They were like, "Baby . . . it's the middle of the day." I got back to my room, and later, the surgeon came in and said the words no one wants to hear after surgery: "We ran into a hiccup." A hiccup.

Now, I don't know who started the trend of using cute little words for terrifying medical situations, but I would like a meeting. He explained that, when he went in laparoscopically, my appendix was fused to my intestine. He didn't know if I was born that way or if the infection had caused it, but it wasn't coming off like it should. And then he said—like he was describing a minor home repair—"So I closed you back up, opened you up the 'old-school-way', and handled it."

This is how I learned that "old school" in surgery means: Your body becomes a construction site. I walked away with a scar and a brand-new respect for the phrase, "You don't know what you don't know."

And then, a few years later, I was scrolling social media one weekend—like we all do, for fun and emotional damage—and I saw a story making the rounds about a surgeon who was being accused of a catastrophic mistake in the operating room. It was horrifying. The kind of thing that makes your stomach drop because somebody's family lost someone they loved.

And as I kept reading, the story explained that a surgeon performed a failed laparoscopic procedure in which he had to open the patient up the "old-school-way," and my stomach turned over. Because the name attached to the allegations was . . . the same surgeon who had performed my appendectomy, describing the same issue that happened with my own surgery.

And I just sat there, staring at my phone, thinking: *So I've really been out here living my life after making a cameo on an episode of "Dr. Death."* Now, I'm not here to litigate the Internet or act like I know the full story behind what I saw online. I wasn't in those operating rooms. I don't know all the details. I just know what it feels like to realize you were on a table once, trusting someone with your life, and then later seeing their name connected to something that makes your blood run cold.

It'll make you grateful. It'll make you quiet for a minute. And it'll make you think about what comfort looks like when you've been through something terrifying. For me, when I finally came back to myself—groggy, stitched up, still trying to piece together the last eight hours—do you know what I wanted? Not a steak. Not a salad. Not anything fancy. I wanted grits. Not just any grits, either. I wanted the hospital grits—because that hospital, somehow, had grits that were actually good. And that is rare. That is a miracle on its own.

Grits are humble. They're not flashy. They don't try to impress anybody. They just show up warm and steady and comforting—like a Southern Mamaw patting your hand and saying, "Eat, honey." And when life has sliced you open—literally or figuratively—comfort matters. That's what grits are. They're the food version of "you're going to be okay."

So, in honor of surviving a surgery that turned into a five-hour surprise, in honor of my body's resilience, and in honor of the only thing I could think about afterward . . . Let's talk about grits.

The kind that soothe you. The kind that stick with you. The kind that remind you that sometimes the simplest things are the ones that carry you through.

# Cream Cheese Grits

**SERVES 4 TO 6**

**prep:** 5 minutes | **cook:** 10 to 15 minutes *(depending on your grits)* | **total:** 15 to 20 minutes

*First things first: Grits are a Southern corn porridge that have been feeding hungry people, healing bad days, and holding entire breakfasts together since forever. You could just eat them with eggs, bacon, and toast . . . but you could also build yourself a whole masterpiece: shrimp, sausage, green onions, extra cheese—whatever your heart desires. The key is this: a good grit base. Because once the base is right, everything you put on top is basically icing on the cake, except it's savory . . . and socially acceptable for breakfast.*

**Chicken stock (enough to cook grits per package instructions)**
**Quick-cooking grits, uncooked (NOT instant)**
**Salted butter (start with 1 tablespoon, then follow your spirit)**
**Cream cheese (a good slice—about 2 to 4 ounces, more if you're trying to heal something)**
**Salt and ground black pepper, to taste (optional, depending on how salty your stock is)**
**Extra butter and salt, to serve**

**1. Bring the stock to a boil.** In a medium saucepan, heat your chicken stock according to the liquid amount on your grits package.

**2. Whisk in the grits.** Once the stock is boiling, pour in grits slowly while whisking. Keep whisking for the first minute so you don't end up with gritty golf balls.

**3. Simmer until tender.** Reduce heat to low and cook per package instructions, whisking often so the bottom doesn't scorch and the grits stay creamy.

**4. Make it rich.** When the grits are tender, whisk in 1 tablespoon butter. More butter, more better. This is not a suggestion. This is a lifestyle.

**5. Add the cream cheese.** Add a slice of cream cheese and whisk until fully melted and silky. Taste. Add more cream cheese if your soul says, "keep going."

**6. Taste and adjust.** Add the salt and pepper only if needed—remember, your stock may already be salty. Serve with butter and extra salt and black pepper, if desired.

# Jalapeño Cheese Grits

**SERVES 10 TO 12**

**prep:** 15 minutes | **cook:** 45 minutes | **total:** 1 hour (plus resting)

*If regular grits are Sunday morning in your pajamas, these are Saturday night in your stilettos. They're creamy, cheesy, a little smoky, and just spicy enough to wake up your taste buds without making you cuss (unless you want to). Serve them with sautéed shrimp, fried chicken, smoked sausage, or all by themselves.*

---

**Softened butter (for greasing the baking dish)**
- 1 **(32-ounce) container chicken stock**
- 1¾ **cups uncooked quick-cooking grits (NOT instant)**
- ½ **cup (1 stick) salted butter**
- 1 **medium onion, diced real good**
- 2 **jalapeño peppers, seeded and diced**
- 2 **cloves garlic, pressed or minced**
- 1 **teaspoon smoked paprika**

**Salt and ground black pepper, to taste**
- 2 **cups freshly shredded sharp Cheddar cheese**
- 2 **cups freshly shredded Monterey Jack cheese**
- 4 **large eggs, beaten**

**Chopped cooked bacon, sliced fresh jalapeño, freshly shredded Cheddar cheese**

1. **Preheat and prep.** Preheat your oven to 350°. Lightly grease a 13x9-inch baking dish with butter.
2. **Cook the grits.** Bring the stock to a boil in a large saucepan. Slowly whisk in the grits. Reduce heat to low and simmer 5 minutes, whisking occasionally until thickened. Cover and remove from heat.
3. **Sauté the flavor.** In a large skillet, melt the butter over medium heat. Add the onion and jalapeño and sauté until translucent and tender, about 5 to 7 minutes. Add the garlic and cook 30 seconds until fragrant. Sprinkle in smoked paprika, then season with salt and black pepper.
4. **Combine.** Stir the sautéed mixture into the warm grits. Add the Cheddar and Monterey Jack and stir until melted and smooth.
5. **Temper the eggs.** Slowly stir a few spoonfuls of the warm grits into the beaten eggs (so you don't end up with scrambled egg confetti). Then stir the egg mixture back into the pot until fully incorporated. Taste and adjust the salt and black pepper.
6. **Bake.** Pour into the prepared dish. Cover with foil and bake 45 minutes, or until set.
7. **Serve hot.** Let sit 5 to 10 minutes before scooping. Top with bacon, jalapeño, and Cheddar cheese.

# Fried Grit Cakes with Parmesan Cream Sauce

**SERVES 8 TO 10** *(depending on how "sample-heavy" your kitchen is)*

**prep:** 25 minutes | **cook:** 20 minutes | **total:** about 4 hours *(includes chilling)*

*These are the grits you make when you want folks to think you went to culinary school, even if your actual training came from a little trial-and-error chaos. Crisp, golden grit cakes on the outside, creamy and cheesy on the inside—then you pour a velvety Parmesan cream sauce over the top. Winner, winner, grit-cake dinner.*

**GRIT CAKES**

- **2 cups whole milk**
- **2 cups chicken stock**
- **Salt, to taste**
- **1 cup quick-cooking grits, uncooked (NOT instant)**
- **½ cup freshly shredded sharp Cheddar cheese**
- **Ground black pepper, to taste**
- **Vegetable oil, for frying**
- **3 large eggs**
- **2 tablespoons whole milk (for the egg wash)**
- **2 cups panko breadcrumbs**
- **1 tablespoon Creole seasoning**

**PARMESAN CREAM SAUCE**

- **3 tablespoons salted butter**
- **3 cloves garlic, grated or minced**
- **2 teaspoons Italian seasoning**
- **4 tablespoons all-purpose flour**
- **2 cups chicken stock (or vegetable broth)**
- **¾ cup heavy cream**
- **8 ounces freshly shredded Parmesan cheese (about 2 cups)**
- **1 tablespoon finely chopped fresh parsley**
- **Salt and ground black pepper, to taste**

**MAKE THE GRITS**

**1. Cook the grits.** In a large saucepan over medium-high heat, combine 2 cups milk, chicken stock, and salt. Heat until it just begins to simmer. Reduce heat to medium-low. Slowly stir in the grits, whisking as you go so you don't create lumps. Cover and cook until thickened, about 5 minutes, whisking occasionally. Remove from heat and stir in the Cheddar and pepper until smooth.

**2. Let grits cool.** Spread the grits into a lightly greased baking dish (an 8 x 8-inch dish works great). Smooth the top. Cover and refrigerate at least 3 hours, until firm enough to cut.

**3. Dredge and fry grit cakes.** When you're ready to fry, pour the oil into a large skillet to about ½-inch deep. Heat over medium until shimmering. In a shallow bowl, whisk the eggs and 2 tablespoons milk. In another shallow bowl, combine breadcrumbs and the Creole seasoning. Use a round cookie cutter to cut the chilled grits into cakes. Dip each cake into the egg mixture, then into the breadcrumb mixture. Repeat for a double coat that fries up extra crisp. Fry the cakes in batches, 2 to 3 minutes per side, until golden brown. Transfer to a paper towel–lined plate and let grit cakes cool slightly.

**MAKE THE SAUCE**

**1. Create cheesy goodness.** Melt butter in a large skillet over medium heat. Add garlic and Italian seasoning. Cook until fragrant, about 1 minute. Sprinkle in flour and cook, whisking, until lightly golden, 2 to 3 minutes. Slowly whisk in chicken stock. Bring to a simmer. Cook until slightly thickened, 2 to 3 minutes. Stir in heavy cream and Parmesan until melted and smooth. Remove from heat and stir in the parsley. Season with salt and pepper.

**ASSEMBLE**

**1.** Stack grit cakes high and drizzle with enough sauce to make you happy.

## Kitchen Tips

- Chill time is non-negotiable. Warm grits do not want to be cakes. Warm grits want to be soup.
- Don't crowd the skillet. Overcrowding drops the oil temp, and you'll end up with "sad golden mush" instead of crisp cakes.
- Want them extra fancy? Top with chopped fresh chives, a few microgreens, or a sprinkle of extra Parmesan.
- Make Ahead: You can make and chill the grits mixture up to 24 hours in advance. Cut and bread right before frying for best texture.
- Store: Refrigerate leftover fried cakes in an airtight container up to 3 days. Store sauce separately up to 4 days.
- Reheat: Grit cakes: Oven or air fryer at 375° until crisp again. (Microwave works but . . . you'll lose the crunch, and we didn't work this hard for soggy.) Sauce: Warm gently on the stove over low heat with a splash of broth/cream to loosen.

# Highway 52

A lot of y'all ask me the same questions—usually in my comments, usually right after I've made something with entirely too much butter and an unreasonable amount of joy: "Meghan . . . why are you so positive all the time?"

"Why do you love people like you do?"

"Why and how do you stay so full of light?"

And I normally answer with something cute, because that's my personality and also my coping mechanism. But the real answer? The real answer is heavy.

So, here's your trigger warning: This story includes violence and loss. If today isn't the day for you to read this, I want you to skip ahead and come back when your heart has the space. Because on March 10, 2009, I was a senior in high school—and I was milliseconds away from being in the wrong place at the wrong time in a way that changes you forever.

That day, my mom and I drove to Samson, Alabama, so I could try on gowns at a dear friend's pageant shop. It was one of those sweet, ordinary days—girly and simple. The kind of day where the biggest decision should've been: Do I look better in jewel tone or pastel? I finished trying on dresses, and my mother—doing what mothers do—reached into her purse and realized she'd forgotten her wallet in the car.

She was talking, so she handed me her keys and said, "Hey, go grab my wallet out of the car so I can pay for this." So, I took the keys, walked out of the shop, and headed toward the car. And I need you to understand how normal that moment felt.

No warning. No feeling in the air. No dramatic music. No slow motion. This was a sleepy little town. The most action this town saw was a traffic jam of three vehicles following behind a John Deere tractor going from one field to the next.

Just keys in my hand. A little errand. A simple request. I unlocked the car, grabbed the wallet, shut the door, locked it, and turned right around to walk back inside. I had barely stepped back into the shop—barely let that door close behind me—when we heard a sound that didn't make sense at first. Sharp. Loud. Repeating. At first, your brain doesn't label it correctly, because your brain is kind. Your brain tries to protect you from the truth. So, for a split second, we didn't register what it was. But it didn't take long. Sirens. Commotion. Chaos moving through the air like a wave. Time stopped.

And we later learned what was happening just outside: A young man drove down Highway 52 and opened fire—taking innocent lives. By the end of that day, 10 people were gone, including the shooter.

And I can say it plainly now, but I still feel it in my chest when I think about it: I was standing right there. I was in that intersection. I was in that space—just seconds before. I don't tell you that for drama. I tell you because a close encounter with death rearranges the furniture in your soul. It makes you understand, in a way you can't unknow, that life is fragile. That the difference between "I'm fine" and "everything changes" can be as small as a moment . . . as small as a wallet . . . as small as a door closing behind you.

And when you've seen how quickly life can be taken, you start treating it like the gift it is. That day didn't make me fearless. It made me grateful. It made me soft in the best ways. It made me pay attention.

Here's what I believe: We have been created on purpose, for a purpose. Divinely designed. Divinely assigned. And somewhere along the way, I realized my purpose is tied to serving people. In any way I can. Cooking for them. Feeding them. Making them giggle when their day has been heavy. Encouraging them. Showing up. Giving a smile. Being generous when I can. Being kind even when it would be easier to be cold.

That's where I feel most fulfilled—because I genuinely believe love changes people. And I also believe it's hard to stay negative with a heart full of gratitude. Now, I know "life is a gift" sounds like something stitched on a decorative pillow at Hobby Lobby. I know it's cliché. I get it.

But hear me: When you've been spared—when you've been that close—you start waking up with a different posture. Every morning, I open my eyes and think, *Thank you, God.* Not because everything is easy. Not because nothing hurts. Not because life is perfect. But because I have one more day. One more day to love somebody. One more day to speak life into somebody. One more day to live.

And when you start counting the things you're grateful for, you don't leave much room to camp out in the things that aren't so great. That doesn't mean you never grieve. It doesn't mean you don't have hard days.

It just means gratitude becomes the ground you stand on. And that's also why I have grace for people—because grace has been given to me in ways I didn't earn. So, the least I can do is give it away.

That's my message to you in this chapter: Life is a gift. It is fleeting and fragile. So, when I tell you I love you, I mean it. When I say I'm glad you're here, I mean it. When I say there is still joy to be found, I mean it. Because you have no idea whose life you can change by simply loving and serving them. That's how you change the world. You don't have to be famous. You don't have to be perfect. You just have to love people on purpose. So, you wonder why I'm positive. You wonder why I'm full of joy. It's because I'm alive. And I never want to waste that.

I want to take you about 30 miles west of Samson into a town called Slocomb. Both Slocomb and Samson are part of the same county—Geneva County, Alabama. Now listen . . . Slocomb is known for the best tomatoes in all the country. Not the county—the country. People travel from all over the world to try a Slocomb tomato, and if you've ever had one, you understand why folks talk about them like they're a sacred experience.

In honor of that tiny county with a huge heart, I want to dedicate these recipes to the resilient residents of Geneva County.

The next couple of recipes use an ingredient Geneva County is known for: Slocomb tomatoes—the kind folks will drive a long way for. And you may not be blessed enough to have a true Slocomb tomato in your kitchen, and that's okay. Just think of Geneva County when you take that first bite.

And remember: Every meal is a moment. Every table is a gift. Every day you're here is worth something.

# Tomato Gravy

**SERVES 4 TO 6** ***(depending on biscuit enthusiasm)***

**prep:** 10 minutes | **cook:** 15 to 20 minutes | **total:** 25 to 30 minutes

*Anytime I make bacon, I save the grease. Not because I'm "thrifty," but because I'm Southern. Growing up, my Mamaw kept a little jar of bacon drippings in the fridge like it was liquid gold—because it is. And if you want tomato gravy to taste like it came from somebody's kitchen who means business, you need bacon grease. Can you use butter? Sure. Should you? Eh. This gravy is savory, tangy, comforting, and best served over a hot buttermilk biscuit that's ready to soak up every last bit.*

- 3 tablespoons bacon grease (preferred) or butter
- 1 small sweet onion, finely chopped
- 16 ounces chopped tomatoes (fresh is best—Slocomb if you're blessed; canned works, too)
- 3 tablespoons all-purpose flour
- ¼ cup chicken stock
- ¼ cup heavy cream (optional, for creamier gravy—but whole milk works too)
- Salt and ground black pepper, to taste
- Hot sauce (Tabasco or Crystal), to taste (optional but I love a kick)
- Hot biscuits
- 6 slices cooked bacon

**1. Warm your grease.** In a large skillet over medium heat, melt the bacon grease (or butter).

**2. Soften the onion.** Add the chopped onion and cook 3 to 4 minutes, stirring, until softened and smelling like something good is about to happen.

**3. Add the tomatoes.** Stir in the chopped tomatoes and cook 2 to 3 minutes until they're hot and starting to break down a bit.

**4. Make your slurry (the anti-lump insurance).** In a small bowl, whisk the flour into the chicken stock until completely smooth. No lumps. None. We are not making tomato dumplings today.

**5. Thicken the gravy.** Pour the flour/stock mixture into the skillet, whisking constantly, until fully incorporated.

**6. Boil, then simmer.** Bring the gravy to a gentle boil, then immediately reduce heat to low and simmer 10 minutes, stirring occasionally, until thickened.

**7. Finish it off.** Stir in the heavy cream (if using). Season with the salt, pepper, and a few dashes of hot sauce, if you like a little kick.

**8. Serve it up.** Spoon over hot biscuits, and serve with cooked bacon. Then, enjoy like somebody who knows what they're doing.

## Kitchen Tips

* Bacon grease matters. It adds that deep, savory flavor that butter just can't imitate.
* Fresh vs. canned tomatoes: Fresh gives you brighter flavor; canned is still delicious—just drain a bit if they're extra juicy.
* Want it smoother? Use an immersion blender for a few pulses, or chop the tomatoes smaller to start.
* Add bacon on top if you want to be dramatic.
* Make Ahead: Tomato gravy is best fresh, but you can make it up to 2 days ahead.
* Storage: Refrigerate in airtight container up to 3 days.

# Tomato Pie
## *(A Love Letter to Slocomb Tomatoes)*

SERVES 8

**prep:** 20 minutes | **cook:** 30 minutes *(plus 10 minutes to pre-bake crust)* | **total:** 1 hour 15 minutes *(includes resting)*

*A buttery crust, juicy tomato slices, fresh basil, and a cheesy topping are basically Southern sophistication in one dish. Tomato pie is simple, but it will humble you if you skip the blotting step.*

**TOMATO PIE**

- 1 (9-inch) deep-dish pie crust (homemade or store bought; no judgment, baby)
- 4 to 5 ripe tomatoes
- Salt, for drawing out moisture

**CHEESY TOPPING**

- ¾ cup mayonnnaise
- 1 cup freshly shredded mozzarella cheese
- 1 cup freshly shredded Cheddar cheese
- 2 tablespoons freshly grated Parmesan cheese
- Ground black pepper, to taste
- ¼ cup sliced green onion
- 8 to 10 fresh basil leaves, chopped

**Garnish: chopped fresh basil**

**"I'M FEELING FANCY" FINISH**

**A tiny drizzle of truffle oil (optional)**

**1. Prebake the crust.** Preheat your oven to 350°. Place the piecrust in a pie plate. Then, place pie plate on a baking sheet (for easier handling). Bake for 10 minutes. Set aside.

**2. Prep the tomatoes (aka: defeat the soggy crust).** Slice the tomatoes thin and lay them out on paper towels or a clean kitchen towel. Sprinkle lightly with salt and let them rest 10 minutes to pull moisture out. After resting, blot and gently press each slice with paper towels to remove as much liquid as possible. Don't mash them—just press like you mean it.

**3. Mix the topping.** In a bowl, combine the mayonnaise, mozzarella, Cheddar, Parmesan, black pepper, and green onion. Stir until everything's well mixed and looking like a creamy, cheesy dream.

**4. Assemble.** Arrange blotted tomato slices in the prebaked crust in an even layer (or pretty spirals if you're feeling artistic). Sprinkle the chopped basil over the tomatoes. Dollop the cheese mixture over the top, then spread it to the edges so it covers the tomatoes completely.

**5. Bake.** Bake at 350° for 30 minutes, or until the top is golden and bubbly. Let it rest 15 minutes before slicing—this helps it set and keeps it from sliding into tomato lava. Garnish with chopped fresh basil, if desired.

**6. Optional finish.** Right before serving, drizzle a tiny bit of truffle oil on top.

## Kitchen Tips

- Shred your own cheese. Pre-shredded cheese has anti-caking agents that can mess with your melt. We want silky, not suspicious.
- Blotting is not optional. If you skip it, your crust will weep. And so will you.
- Use ripe tomatoes. Overripe = extra watery = chaos.
- Add-ins (if you want): a pinch of red pepper flakes, a few crumbles of bacon, or a thin layer of Dijon mustard on the crust before tomatoes for a little tang.
- Make Ahead: You can prebake the crust up to 1 day ahead. You can slice/salt/blot tomatoes up to 2 hours ahead (keep them layered between paper towels in the fridge).
- Storage: Refrigerate leftovers in an airtight container up to 3 days.
- Reheating: Best reheated in the oven at 350° for 10 to 12 minutes to keep the crust crisp. Microwaving works, but it will soften the crust (and I will still love you, but I will be a little sad).

# 3

# Southern Porch Party

This chapter is for the gatherers. The ones who know that a good dip can hold a room together, that cheese is a love language, and that sometimes the best memories start with "Well, we didn't really have a plan, but everybody showed up anyway." Inside these pages, you'll find party food with a whole lot of personality, but this chapter isn't really just about delicious appetizers. It's about the people who fill the room. The friends who become family, and the strangers who turn into stories.

# The Richest Woman in the World

The state of Florida was about 27 inches behind on rain. And naturally—because the weather has a sense of humor and a personal vendetta against hosts—all 27 inches decided to arrive on the exact day I was hosting a huge Christmas party. Not a little get-together. Not "drop by if you're in the area." A party-party. The kind of party you plan like a production. The kind you build your whole week around. The kind you decorate for like the Internet is coming, even if the Internet is not, in fact, coming. This party mattered.

We had just moved into our new, forever home—the one you pray for, the one you build dreams around, the one you walk through at night and still can't believe is yours. And I had decorated it so intentionally and so perfectly that I'm pretty sure Martha Stewart's spirit would've whispered, "Okay, queen."

We had a 15-foot Christmas tree in the corner—15 feet of holiday confidence—gussied to the gills with ornaments and ribbon and twinkle lights. It wasn't just a tree. It was an announcement. It was a testimony.

And we invited everybody we love. Family. Friends. Our people. The ones we want to celebrate the season with under one roof—the ones who've held pieces of our story. Now, here's the thing about me: I cook everything. Because that's what I do.

Cooking is my love language. Cooking is the way I say, "I'm glad you're here," without having to stare into someone's eyes for too long and get emotional. Cooking is how I make love tangible.

So, I cooked. All day. I cooked like I was feeding a small village and trying to earn a badge for it. I cooked because the only thing I fear more than awkward silence is running out of food. When you host a party, your job is to feed people and entertain people—and I take that job personally. I don't want anyone leaving my house hungry. I don't want someone looking at the spread and thinking, *Bless her heart, she tried.* No ma'am. If you come to my home, you will be fed.

Three days before the party, I checked the forecast: 87% chance of rain. *Well,* I thought, *that's . . . promising.* Because in my mind, I was clinging to the remaining 13% like it was faith.

The day of the party came and the forecast said 100%. Not just 100%—the weather app had the audacity to add details: One to two inches expected. That's not "a little rain." That's a downpour. That's a baptism. That's "the animals are lining up two by two."

And then the thought hit me—the thought that every host has had at least once: Nobody is going to come.

Because here's the other factor: We live out on our farm now, about 25 miles outside of town. It's not hard for me anymore—I've accepted it as a small sacrifice for a big reward. But other people haven't figured that out yet. Not everybody wants to drive out to the country in the dark in the rain, especially during the holidays when everybody is already tired and over-scheduled and emotionally fragile.

So, I stood there in my pretty house, with my giant tree and my carefully placed decor and my counters covered in food, and I thought: *Well. This is going to be me, my husband, and 70 pounds of leftovers.*

Which—let's be honest—there are worse fates.

But still.

The party started at 5:00 p.m. By that point, I had been preparing all day. I was in full host mode—hair done,

candles lit, music on, food staged like it had a manager.

I was ready and waiting. And . . . a car pulled up. Then, another. Then, another. People started trickling in—family after family, friend after friend—wet hair, umbrellas, wrapped gifts in hand, wiping their shoes on the mat like they were entering a warm little Christmas movie.

And I just kept doing what hosts do. Setting food out. Hugging necks. Mingling. Accepting gifts. Laughing. Refilling drinks. Making sure everybody had a plate.

Living in the moment so fully I didn't even know where my phone was, I couldn't have checked it if you paid me. I was busy being present. And somewhere between the laughter and the clinking cups and the smell of party food and perfume and Christmas tree, the rain became background noise—like it couldn't get in.

Around 7:00 p.m., I finally paused long enough to look up. I looked around at my home. And y'all . . . every person we invited had come. Every one. Not most. Not "the close friends." Not "the ones who live nearby." All of them.

It was a big list, too—70-plus people. And they were all there, packed into our forever home, laughing and talking and eating like the weather had not tried to ruin the night. And I felt it rise in my chest like a wave. That emotion you weren't expecting. That sudden lump in your throat when your heart catches up to what your eyes are seeing.

Because in that moment, I realized something: I wasn't looking at "a party." I was looking at my whole life.

All the different versions of me through all my seasons—adolescence, college years, work years, grown-up years—standing in the same space. People who had loved me when I was awkward and figuring it out. People who had cheered for me when I was brave. People who had carried me when I was tired. People who had been steady when life was not.

All in one room. And for a moment, I felt like the richest woman in the world. Not because of the house. Not because of the tree. Not because the food turned out (though, *thank you, Jesus*). But because community is wealth. Showing up is love. And the fact that 70 people looked at a weather forecast that said "monsoon," looked at a drive that said "25 miles," and still thought, *I'm going . . . because she matters to me*—that will humble you. That will soften you. That will make you grateful in a way you can't manufacture.

Sometimes, we think people won't come. We assume we're a burden. We assume everyone is too busy. We assume our invitation is optional.

But that night reminded me: The right people don't just show up when it's easy. They show up when it's inconvenient. They show up when it's raining. They show up when the road is dark. They show up because love doesn't need perfect conditions.

Love just needs a door to walk through. And that's what parties are, when you strip away the cute details. They're not about impressing anybody. They're about making space. They're about saying, "Come in. Sit down. Eat something. Let me love you for a few hours." That's why I cooked so much. That's why I worried about running out. Because food has always been my way of holding people close.

Not with perfection. With generosity. With warmth. With "Here, take another plate," and "Do you need anything?" and "I'm so glad you made it." So, the following recipes are for *that* kind of gathering. The one where the forecast is ugly, but the night is beautiful. The one where you're tired, but your heart is full. The one where you realize community is the true centerpiece.

We're rolling into party foods now—the dips and bites and little plates that keep hands busy and conversation flowing. The kind of food you can set out and walk away from while you hug necks and laugh and soak it all in. Because when people show up—really show up—you don't need perfection. You just need a table. And something good to put on it.

# THE Cheesy Bread

**SERVES 8 TO 10**

**prep:** 10 to 15 minutes | **cook:** 18 to 20 minutes | **total:** 30 to 35 minutes

*This is THE Cheesy Bread. The one you set on the counter "for everyone" and then catch yourself "sampling" until half the loaf is mysteriously gone. It's buttery, garlicky, oniony, cheesy. Serve it with pasta, soup, salad . . . or just stand over the sink like a gremlin. No judgment here.*

---

- **1 loaf French bread or Italian bread, sliced lengthwise**
- **½ cup (1 stick) salted butter, softened**
- **½ cup mayonnaise**
- **1 teaspoon Worcestershire sauce**
- **3 to 6 cloves garlic, minced (or 27, if you're living your truth)**
- **4 green onions, thinly sliced**
- **½ teaspoon onion powder**
- **½ teaspoon garlic powder**
- **½ teaspoon smoked paprika**
- **Dash of salt**
- **A cracklin' of black pepper**
- **¾ cup freshly grated Parmesan cheese**
- **1½ cups freshly shredded sharp Cheddar cheese**
- **½ cup freshly shredded mozzarella cheese**

**1. Prep the bread and oven.** Place the bread halves on a large rimmed baking sheet. Choose your adventure: Bake method: Preheat oven to 350°. Broil method: Set broiler to LOW.

**2. Make the cheesy spread.** In a bowl, whisk together the softened butter, mayonnaise, and Worcestershire until smooth.

**3. Season it up.** Stir in the garlic, green onions, onion powder, garlic powder, smoked paprika, salt, and pepper.

**4. Fold in the cheese.** Add the Parmesan, Cheddar, and mozzarella, and fold until everything is combined and thick and glorious.

**5. Dollop that cheese.** Spread the cheese mixture all over the cut sides of the bread—edge to edge. Don't be shy.

**6. Bake or broil.** Bake until hot and melty, 18 to 20 minutes. Or, broil until golden and bubbly, 7 to 8 minutes. Keep an eye on it—broilers will turn on you like an ex.

**7. Slice and serve.** Let it sit for 2 minutes so the cheese sets just enough to cut without sliding into the next zip code.

# Swine Shots

SERVES ABOUT 24

**prep:** 20 minutes | **cook:** about 45 minutes | **total:** 1 hour 10 minutes (*includes resting*)

*Smoky sausage is wrapped in bacon, filled with a spicy-cheesy cloud, topped with jalapeño, then glazed in a sweet BBQ drizzle that tastes like summer and bad decisions (the fun kind). Make these once, and you'll be asked to bring them to every occassion . . . forever.*

BBQ DRIZZLE

½ cup barbecue sauce (any brand)
⅛ cup honey
2 teaspoons light brown sugar

SWINE SHOTS

1 pound smoked sausage
1 pound thick-cut bacon
4 ounces cream cheese, room temperature
¼ cup sour cream
½ cup freshly shredded sharp Cheddar cheese
½ teaspoon barbecue seasoning or Cajun seasoning*
4 medium jalapeños, sliced (seeded for less heat)

MAKE THE DRIZZLE

**1. Make the BBQ.** In a small bowl, stir together barbecue sauce, honey, and brown sugar until smooth. Set aside.

MAKE THE SWINE SHOTS

**1. Prep your oven.** Preheat your oven to 375°. Line a large rimmed baking sheet with foil, and set a wire rack on top if you've got one (keeps the bottoms from sitting in grease).

**2. Build the bacon cups.** Slice smoked sausage into thick rounds—about 1 to 1¼ inch. Cut bacon strips in half. Wrap each sausage round with a half-strip of bacon, making a little "cup" with a bit of space above the sausage inside. Secure with a toothpick.

**3. Mix the filling.** In a medium bowl, mix together cream cheese, sour cream, Cheddar, and seasoning until smooth and spreadable. Spoon into a piping bag; or into a resealable plastic bag, and snip off one corner to make a small hole.

**4. Fill 'em up.** Pipe the filling into the top of each swine shot, filling it just to the rim.

**5. Top them.** Place a jalapeño slice on top of each filled swine shot. Drizzle a little BBQ Drizzle over each one.

**6. Bake the shots.** Bake until the bacon is deeply browned and crisp and the filling is bubbly, about 45 minutes.

**7. Rest and serve.** Let them rest 5 minutes before serving. They're molten. Respect the molten. Discard toothpicks. Lightly brush around the edges with any remaining BBQ drizzle, if desired.

**I use Bad Byron's Butt Rub or Slap Ya Mama.*

# Pimiento Cheese

SERVES 8 TO 10

**prep:** 15 minutes | **total:** 15 minutes

*This Pimiento Cheese is sharp, smoky, creamy, and just boujee enough with Parmesan cheese to make it feel "elevated," but still relaxed enough to belong on a saltine. If you really want to take it over the top, keep reading—because smoked sausage plus pepper jelly turns this into a full-blown event.*

- **4 ounces cream cheese, softened**
- **½ cup mayonnaise**
- **1 tablespoon Dijon mustard**
- **1 tablespoon Worcestershire sauce**
- **½ teaspoon garlic powder**
- **½ teaspoon smoked paprika**
- **Salt and ground black pepper, to taste**
- **4 ounce jar pimientos, drained, plus 1 tablespoon pimiento juice**
- **1½ cups freshly shredded sharp Cheddar cheese**
- **¾ cup freshly grated Parmesan cheese**
- **Crackers, fresh vegetables, smoked sausage, and pickled okra, to serve**

**1. Make the creamy base.** In a large mixing bowl, stir together the cream cheese, mayonnaise, Dijon, Worcestershire, garlic powder, smoked paprika, salt, and pepper. Stir together until fully combined.

**2. Add the pimientos.** Stir in the pimientos and 1 tablespoon pimiento juice. Mix well.

**3. Add the cheeses.** Fold in the freshly shredded Cheddar and Parmesan until everything is evenly coated and gorgeous.

**4. Chill (optional, but recommended).** You can eat it immediately (and you will), but if you let it chill 30 minutes, the flavors settle in and act like they have home training. Serve with crackers, fresh vegetables, smoked sausage, and pickled okra.

## Kitchen Tips

* Shred your own cheese. Preshredded cheese has added anti-caking agents, and they mess with the texture.
* Want it smoother? Mix longer, or use a hand mixer for the base before adding the cheese.
* Make it like Luci: Add a pinch of cayenne pepper or diced jalapeño.
* Make Ahead: Make up to 3 days in advance. Flavor gets even better.
* Store: Covered in the fridge for 4 to 5 days.
* Do not freeze: The texture can get weird once thawed. Pimiento cheese deserves stability.

**Bonus: The Snack Stack That Will Ruin Your Self-Control.**

* Smoked Sausage + Pimiento Cheese + Pepper Jelly Bites = Heaven
* You'll need: smoked link sausage (grilled and sliced), crackers, pepper jelly, pimiento cheese
* Assemble in this order: Cracker, sausage slice, dollop of pimiento cheese, and finish with a spoonful of pepper jelly on top. That's not a snack. That's a statement.

# Scare Competition

Here is your trigger warning: if you suffer from secondhand embarrassment, please turn the page. Not because this story is scary—because I am.

In my previous job, we worked out of an old historic home. You know the kind: creaky floors, dramatic doorways, and a vibe that says, "This place has secrets . . . and at least one ghost named Joseph." People swore it was haunted. I have arguments both for and against that theory. (For: The lights flickered. Against: We were in a historic house with wiring older than my Papaw's Hardee's crew.)

There were six women and one man in the office. Which means, statistically, there was no peace. Not ever. One day—because we had full access to free will and chose chaos—we decided to start a scaring war.

Now listen. I love a good scare. I love being startled. I love the adrenaline. I love the way it makes your soul briefly leave your body and then come back like, *"Well . . . that was unnecessary."* So, when my male coworker and one of the girls scared the absolute mess out of me coming out of the bathroom, I laughed . . . and then I went spiritually blank.

Because in my mind, the rules were clear:

1. You scare me?
2. I haunt you.

And I don't mean metaphorically. I decided right then and there: Sir, you have opened Pandora's box, and I will not be going quietly into the night. I will be *waiting*. I will be *watching*. I will be *marinating*.

A couple weeks went by. Because I am patient. I can play the long game. I can hold a grudge like a cast-iron skillet holds flavor. It was a Tuesday. All the girls were in the office. And it was customary for my male coworker to stroll in around 8:30 a.m. like a man who has never been humbled by a jump scare in his life. I heard him unlock his office. I heard him settle in. And I thought, *Today's the day.*

Because I knew his schedule. Mid-morning, like clockwork, he'd take a bathroom break. And I knew that once he headed that way, I'd have about—oh—26 minutes to get in position, mentally prepare, and become a problem. Now, here's the layout: To get to the bathroom, you had to go through the stairwell and cross into a little room on the other side. Perfect. A threshold. A dramatic entrance. A stage. A place where a grown man could lose years off his life.

So I waited. I heard the footsteps. Game time. I slipped into the stairwell like a Southern ninja. I got into position. I heard the toilet flush. I heard him wash his hands—because he is a decent human being. I heard the door open. And I thought, *Showtime.*

The second a toe crossed that threshold, I launched. I hollered. I screamed. I made sounds I didn't even know I had access to. I am telling you: It was belligerent. It was theatrical. It was the kind of scare that would've made Universal Studios call me and say, "Hey . . . you busy this fall?" It was the best scare I have ever delivered. I looked up, fully expecting to see my coworker folded like a lawn chair.

And what I saw instead was . . . a little old lady. Friends. She was maybe 5 feet 1 inch and 90 pounds soaking wet. The kind of woman who probably has a purse full of peppermints and wisdom. The kind of woman who says, "Oh my lands" unironically.

And mid-scream, my brain finally caught up and said, *Meghan . . . that is not him.* Time slowed down. I realized I had just unleashed a full-volume demon impression on a stranger. So—because I apparently panic like a raccoon—I did the only thing my body could think to do: I hugged her.

Why did I hug her? She was a stranger. I had just scared her into another dimension. There was no reason for a hug. But I think my brain was like, *"If we embrace her, maybe this becomes a greeting and not a felony."* This tiny woman let out a holler that proved she had incredible lung capacity. It was impressive. Honestly, she could've led worship.

And I'm standing there holding her like, "I'm so sorry. I'm so sorry. I'm so sorry." And she's looking at me like, "Ma'am, what demon are you and why do you work here?"

Finally, I stammer out, "What . . . what are you doing here?" And she says—shaking, clutching her purse, probably seeing her whole life flash before her—"I came to fill out a membership application for your organization."

And I—still in shock, still holding onto her like we're cousins at a funeral—said, "Well . . . welcome to the team."

Then, she hits me with the one sentence that made my soul fully exit my body: "I do have a heart condition."

Of course you do. Because why wouldn't you. And if you didn't before, I'm pretty sure I just gifted you one in the stairwell of a haunted office.

So now, I'm switching personalities at record speed. I go from Mike Wazowski to Florence Nightingale. I'm watching her like a hawk for signs of cardiac distress, because I can't even run away from what I've done. I'm locked into the consequences.

I sat with her until I knew she was okay. Which is a very specific kind of awkward: *Hey, I just scared the life out of you. So, I'm going to sit here and monitor your vitals with my eyes. Would you like a water? A prayer? A waiver?*

And that, my friends, is what it's like to be around me: I will accidentally ruin your day . . . and then I will love you through it.

And here's the kitchen lesson (because yes, we are taking this back to food): There are two places you do not move with arrogance:

1. A stairwell in a "maybe haunted" historic house
2. A kitchen full of sharp objects and hot grease

Because the moment you get too confident—when you start thinking, *I've got this, I don't need to be careful, I'm a seasoned pro*—that is when life humbles you. Sometimes with a mandoline slicer. Sometimes with a stranger. Sometimes with both in the same week.

So, whether you're planning a scare, or planning supper: Pay attention to what you're doing, know who's walking through the doorway, and don't let your pride be louder than your common sense.

Speaking of unexpected guests and me learning lessons the hard way—let's get back to the kitchen, where the only thing I'm trying to scare today is a vegetable.

# Lasagna Dip

**SERVES 8 TO 10**

**prep:** 15 minutes | **cook:** 15 minutes
**total:** 30 minutes

*Sometimes, you want lasagna, but you do not want to babysit noodles, layer like you're building a brick house, and then wait an hour to eat. This dip is for those moments. It's cheesy, saucy, sausage-y, and absolutely illegal with toasted bread. Think: lasagna's fun cousin who shows up late, steals the spotlight, and leaves with your chips.*

CHEESE LAYER

**1½ cups freshly shredded mozzarella cheese**
**¾ cup freshly grated Parmesan cheese**
**16 ounces whole-milk ricotta cheese**

SAUCE LAYER

**2 tablespoons olive oil**
**1 pound ground Italian sausage (mild or hot)**
**2 teaspoons garlic powder**
**1 teaspoon dried thyme**
**1 teaspoon dried parsley**
**Salt and ground black pepper, to taste**
**1 (24-ounce) jar marinara sauce**

BIG FINISH

**1 cup freshly shredded mozzarella cheese (for topping)**
**Garnish: fresh basil leaves, torn or chopped**

**1. Preheat and prep.** Preheat your oven to 425°. Grab an 8x8-inch baking dish.

**2. Cheese layer.** In a large bowl, whisk together 1½ cups mozzarella, Parmesan, and ricotta until combined. Set aside.

**3. Sauce layer.** In a large skillet, add olive oil and sausage, and cook over medium-high heat until browned and crumbled. Stir in garlic powder, thyme, parsley, salt, and pepper. Pour in the marinara sauce, stir, and let it simmer for a few minutes to get cozy.

**4. Layer Like Lasagna (But Easier).** In your baking dish, layer in thirds:

- ⅓ sauce in the bottom
- ⅓ cheese mixture (dollop and spread gently)
- ⅓ sauce
- ⅓ cheese mixture
- ⅓ sauce
- final ⅓ cheese mixture

**5. Make it cheesey.** Sprinkle the additional 1 cup mozzarella evenly over the top.

**6. Bake.** Bake until hot, bubbly, and acting brand new, 15 minutes,

**7. Finish.** Pull it out of the oven, and immediately sprinkle with fresh basil.

# Fried Dill Pickle Dip

**SERVES 8 TO 10**

**prep:** 10 minutes | **cook:** 5 minutes
**total:** 2 hours 15 minutes

*If you've ever eaten a fried pickle and thought,* I wish this was a personality trait, *this dip is for you. It's creamy, tangy, ranchy, and topped with buttery toasted breadcrumbs that taste like the crispy coating you fight over in the basket. Serve it at a party, and watch folks hover like seagulls at a beach picnic.*

TOASTED TOPPING

**1 tablespoon salted butter**
**½ cup plain panko breadcrumbs**

PICKLE DIP

**8 ounces cream cheese, softened**
**1 cup sour cream**
**1 tablespoon dill pickle juice**
**2 tablespoons ranch seasoning mix or 1 (1-ounce) ranch seasoning mix packet**
**¼ teaspoon garlic powder**
**Salt and freshly ground black pepper, to taste**
**1 cup dill pickles, finely chopped (try not to "sample" half the cup)**

**Garnish: toasted breadcrumbs, chopped fresh dill (optional but adorable)**

**1. Toasted topping.** In a small skillet, melt the butter over medium heat. Add the breadcrumbs, and stir constantly until golden brown and toasty, about 3 to 5 minutes. Remove from heat, and let cool.

**2. Mix the dip.** In a large bowl, whip together the cream cheese and sour cream using an elextric mixer at medium-low speed until smooth and creamy.

**3. Season it.** Add pickle juice, ranch seasoning, garlic powder, salt, and pepper. Mix again until fully combined. Stir in the chopped pickles until evenly distributed.

**4. Chill.** Spread the dip into a serving dish, cover, and refrigerate for at least 2 hours so the flavors can get to know each other properly.

**5. Finish and serve.** Right before serving, top with a generous shower of toasted breadcrumbs and a little fresh dill if you're feeling fancy.

# Bacon Swiss Dip

**SERVES 8 TO 10**

**prep:** 15 minutes | **cook:** 35 minutes
**total:** 1 hour (*includes cooling*)

*This dip is proof that bacon and cheese can solve most problems. It's rich, salty, melty, and topped with buttery crackers that get all golden around the edges like they're doing the Lord's work.*

**1 pound center-cut bacon, chopped**
**1 sleeve buttery round crackers,* crushed (plus a few "quality control" crackers, naturally)**
**16 ounces cream cheese, softened**
**2½ teaspoons garlic powder**
**2 teaspoons onion powder**
**Salt and ground black pepper, to taste**
**8 ounces freshly shredded Swiss cheese**

**1. Preheat.** Preheat your oven to 375°. Lightly spray an 8x8-inch baking dish with cooking spray.
**2. Cook the bacon.** In a medium skillet, cook chopped bacon over medium heat until crispy. Important note: once bacon goes into cheese and bakes, it softens. So if you think it's done, cook it a bit longer. Drain on paper towels.
**3. Get out that frustration.** Keep the crackers in the sleeve. Put a hand on each end and smash inward like you're compressing your feelings. Voilà—crumbs.
**4. Mix it up.** In a mixing bowl (or right in the warm pan if you're careful), combine cream cheese bacon, garlic powder, onion powder, salt, and pepper. Mix until it's well combined and the bacon is evenly distributed. Fold in Swiss until it's fully mixed in.
**5. Bake it.** Spread the mixture into your prepared dish. Sprinkle the crushed crackers around the edges. Bake until hot, bubbly, and lightly golden where it counts, about 35 minutes. Let it sit for 5 to 10 minutes before serving—because molten cheese is delicious, but it will remove a layer of skin if you get too excited.

**I used Ritz crackers.*

# Boursin Dip

**SERVES 8 TO 10**

*Make this when you want people to think you did the most . . . but you actually did the least.*

**prep:** 5 minutes | **cook:** 0 minutes
**total:** 5 minutes

**1 (5.2-ounce) package garlic-herb cheese spread***
**⅓ to ½ cup fig preserves**
**2 to 3 tablespoons hot honey***
**¼ cup pistachios, chopped**
**Vegetables, to serve**

**1. Spoon and spread.** Spoon the cheese spread onto a serving plate or shallow bowl, and spread it into an even layer.
**2. Top it off.** Dollop the fig preserves over the top, and gently spread. Drizzle with hot honey.
**3. Finish with crunch.** Sprinkle chopped pistachios over everything. Serve immediately with vegetables or whatever vehicle you've got nearby.

**I use Boursin Garlic & Fine Herbs and Mike's Hot Honey.*

# Green Street Prom

Green Street Prom was born the way all truly iconic college decisions are born: With absolutely no adult supervision and a dangerously optimistic belief that you are the first person on earth to ever have a good idea.

In college, my best friends and I lived in the same apartment quadplex on Green Street—four little units clustered together like a theatrical commune. We were chosen family. Most of us were theater majors. All dramatic by trade and by temperament. We survived on caffeine, community, and the kind of delusion it takes to believe you can live completely on ramen and 57 frozen pizzas and still be emotionally available.

Our doors were always open. Somebody was always cooking something. Somebody was always rehearsing lines in the hallway like it was normal. Somebody was always crying—usually over a boy, a grade, or a monologue that "just wasn't landing." And somehow, in the middle of all that chaos, we were the happiest we'd ever been.

We didn't have much money. But we had each other. And honestly? That is the richest kind of life. One random day—freshmen year, when you still think you're invincible and sleep is optional—we looked around at the little quadplex kingdom and thought: *What if we throw a prom?* Now . . . we were not going to an actual prom. We were not invited to a fancy ballroom.

There was no fundraiser. No formal. No charity gala. No "special occasion" on the calendar that justified anything we were about to do.

We just wanted to dress up, eat well, and probably drink a little more than we should—because we were 19 and believed hydration was a myth. And the thing about theater people is . . . we don't need a reason. We need a *theme*. So we named it Green Street Prom, like that alone made it a tradition with historical significance. Like it was going to be written about in future textbooks: "And on this sacred night, the drama majors gathered in polyester and dreams."

The girls all had prom dresses still hanging in their closets—beautiful gowns we wore once, and then preserved like artifacts. You know the ones: still in the garment bag, still holding on to a scent of cheap celebrity perfume and teenage optimism.

And we were itching for an excuse to wear them again. So we did. We got gussied up for no reason whatsoever—which is, in my opinion, the purest reason of all.

We curled hair. We pinned bobby pins like we were constructing an architectural masterpiece. We did our makeup with the intensity of people preparing for the red carpet . . . and the red carpet was actually a slightly sticky apartment floor we had mopped "good enough."

Somebody put on music. Somebody lit candles that absolutely should not have been around college boys. Somebody yelled, "Is this too much?" and the rest of us answered in unison, "NOT ENOUGH."

We had food—because of course we did. We didn't throw parties, we threw events. We weren't feeding people snacks; we were feeding people feelings.

We had a theme, too, because theater majors cannot simply "hang out." We must create an immersive experience.

We set up a photo booth, complete with props that were either borrowed, thrifted, or stolen from the deepest corner of someone's trunk. We even took an obligatory group photo on the staircase—lined up like a cast photo, grinning like we were starring in something big.

And we were. Because that night wasn't about prom. It was about permission. Permission to celebrate without earning it. Permission to be joyful without waiting for life to "calm down." Permission to use the good plates and wear the fancy dress and light the candles and make the meal just because you're alive and together and breathing.

We spend so much of life saving the good stuff. Saving the nice outfit for "someday." Saving the good china for "a special occasion." Saving the fancy dinner for "when we have more money." Saving the celebration for "when things are better."

But the truth is . . . you don't always get a trumpet blast announcing the special days. Sometimes, you have to make them special on purpose. Sometimes, the occasion is just: We're here. We're young. We're loved. We made it through another week. We're together. We have laughter in our lungs and music in the living room and a dress that deserves to see the light of day again. And that is worth celebrating. That's what I learned on Green Street. Life is not a waiting room. Life is the party.

Not every party needs a fancy venue. Some of the best ones happen in the middle of ordinary life—when you decide to stop rushing past it and actually taste it.

So, if you're reading this and you've been saving the good china, honey . . . pull it out. If you've been waiting for a reason to wear the dress, put it on.

If you've been holding your joy like it's fragile, I'm here to tell you: Joy is meant to be used. Every breath is a reason to celebrate. And the truth is, the moments we remember most aren't always the "big" ones.

They're the ones we created out of nothing. The ones we made beautiful on purpose. So, let this be your sign: Throw the party. Light the candles. Make the meal. Take the picture. Laugh too loud. Dance in your living room like the whole world isn't watching—because the right people will never make you feel silly for celebrating.

And if anyone asks what the occasion is? Look them dead in the eye and say: "Green Street Prom."

Because, sometimes, the most magical nights are the ones you didn't wait for. You just lived them.

"Turn up the heat:
Use hot honey."
*—Luci*

# Mini Cranberry, Pecan & Goat Cheese Truffles

**SERVES 32** ***(depending on scoop size)***

**prep:** 20 minutes | **total:** 20 minutes (*plus 2 hours chilling*)

*These little truffles are what happens when a cheese board and a holiday dessert fall in love. They're creamy, sweet, tangy, crunchy, and fancy looking—without requiring fancy effort. Set them out with warm crostini and watch folks flock to them.*

- **10 ounces goat cheese, softened**
- **6 ounces cream cheese, softened**
- **3 tablespoons honey, plus more for drizzling the tops**
- **2 teaspoons ground cinnamon**
- **1 teaspoon ground nutmeg**
- **1½ cups pecans, finely chopped, divided**
- **1 cup dried cranberries, finely chopped**
- **½ cup finely chopped fresh parsley**

**1. Make the filling.** In a large bowl, beat together the goat cheese, cream cheese, honey, cinnamon, and nutmeg with an electric mixer at medium-high speed until light and fluffy. Fold in ½ cup chopped pecans.

**2. Make the coating.** Line your counter with parchment paper. In the center of the parchment, toss together the cranberries, parsley, and remaining 1 cup pecans.

**3. Scoop and roll.** Using a large cookie scoop (or a 1-tablespoon scoop), scoop the cheese mixture into balls, and roll each one in the cranberry-pecan-parsley coating until fully covered. Refrigerate until firm, about 2 hours. When ready to serve, drizzle with honey.

## Kitchen Tips

* Softened cheese matters. Let the goat cheese and cream cheese sit at room temp for 20 to 30 minutes so they whip up smooth.
* Too sticky? Pop the filling in the fridge for 10 to 15 minutes, then roll again.
* Want them extra pretty? Finish with a light honey drizzle right before serving.
* Make Ahead: Up to 2 days in advance.
* Storage: In an airtight container in the fridge.
* Serve: Best slightly chilled but let them sit out 10 minutes if you want them extra creamy.

# The Pond

When I was in college, my fellow theater majors and I had a sacred tradition every Thursday night. Not a healthy tradition or a financially responsible tradition. A sacred one.

We'd pile into whatever vehicles would start that night and drive 45 minutes to the nearest restaurant chain for half-priced appetizers, which, if you really sit and think about it, made no sense at all. Because we would spend the cost of the "other half" in gas money to get there.

But logic has never been the point of theater people. The point is the ritual. The point is the drama. The point is sitting in a booth with your chosen family, still wearing stage makeup in places it doesn't belong, ordering spinach-artichoke dip like you just survived a war (which, emotionally, you did).

We'd walk in loud, hungry, and slightly feral from rehearsal—our hair pinned up in ways that were either "period accurate" or "just gave up," our voices hoarse from singing the same measures a hundred times, and our bodies smelling faintly of sweat, hairspray, and that weird theater smell that never fully leaves your soul.

And every week, we'd say the same thing: "Okay, we're just going to get half-priced appetizers." As if we weren't about to treat that menu like a free-for-all. Oh, and the restaurant had karaoke, too. Which is every theater major's favorite hobby.

Meanwhile, the waitress was looking at our table like, *Oh, I have the theater kids tonight. Lord, strengthen me.*

And somewhere in the middle of all that fried food and laughter and retelling rehearsal disasters like we were live-vlogging our own chaos . . . there was always one person who reminded me what excellence looks like: Kayla.

Kayla is one of the most talented people I have ever known. Truly. She's beautiful, she's funny, the total package—the kind of person who walks into a room and you're like, *There she is.*

She's also the kind of friend who inspires you to always do your best . . . because Kayla doesn't know how to do anything halfway. And I'm going to tell you why.

Back in the 2010s, all of us in theater together were tight-knit best friends, the kind of group that could survive tech week and still make each other laugh. (For non-theater people, tech week was where all majors were tested. The week before opening night, we would spend hours going over all the lights, sounds, sets, and costumes.) We were the kind of theater family where somebody always had bobby pins, somebody always had snacks, and somebody was always one inconvenience away from crying in a hallway.

One season, we all auditioned for an original children's show—loosely based on Aesop's fables—written by our favorite choreographer, Manasco. And when I say "written by," I mean he put his whole creative heart into it. It was whimsical, hilarious, and somehow deeply dramatic, because of course it was. Manasco had a gift for making us do things we didn't know were possible—physically and emotionally—and he did the same thing with this script.

It also meant there wasn't really a clear list of dream roles. It was more like a magical hodgepodge of animals, morals, and whatever Manasco had in his brain at 2 a.m. when inspiration struck.

We auditioned. We sang. We read. We did our best "I am a hare learning a valuable lesson" faces. And then, we waited for the cast list.

If you've never experienced cast list posting day, let me explain: It is the most dramatic piece of paper to ever exist. Grown people will act like that list is a life sentence. We all ran back to the theater at post time, hearts racing, scanning for our names like we were searching for survivors.

Everybody's doing that thing where you pretend you don't care but your eyes are moving at the speed of light. And then Kayla steps up to the paper. She finds her name. And beside it, in black and white, the role reads: THE POND.

Now . . . I did not know you could be cast as a literal body of water. I did not know "pond" was a character option. I didn't know we were out here assigning *ecosystems*. But somehow—some way—Kayla had been cast as a freaking pond.

A POND. Not a princess. Not the clever hare. Not the narrator with cute lines. Not even a supporting chicken. No. Water. Still water. With vibes. And the costume? Y'all.

They strapped a kiddie pool to her BACK. A full-sized plastic kiddie pool. Like something turtles live in.

Like she was about to carry a small family of ducks to safety. She had to stand up with it. She had to lay down with it. She had to move, act, speak, and perform while wearing what can be described as a portable splash zone.

It was strenuous. It was absurd. It was the kind of costume that makes you question theater as an art form and also as a lifestyle choice. And I will never forget one of the funniest things that ever came out of her mouth. Someone would ask her, "What were you cast as?" And Kayla—dead serious, with the confidence of a woman announcing a lead role on Broadway—goes: "Oh, me? I'm THE POND."

I don't remember what parts half the rest of us played. I truly don't. But what I *do* remember is Kayla slayed every line. Oceans were jealous of her commitment. Rivers were threatened. The Everglades took notes.

She stole the show as a pond. And that's the part that still gets me—because Kayla could've seen that cast list and said, "Absolutely not. I refuse. I will not be a freaking pond." She could've rolled her eyes and let "pond" be a joke.

But she didn't. She put her whole self into it. She strapped that pool on her back and acted like she was the most important body of water in the Southeastern United States. And because she did, *everybody* remembers it.

To this day, people don't talk about the plot. They talk about Kayla. As the pond. That's the lesson right there. Always do your best. Even when you didn't get the role you pictured. Even when the part feels small, silly, or downright ridiculous. Especially then.

Because there are no small parts—just small actors. And Kayla? Kayla is not small. Not in talent, not in heart, not in effort. She's the kind of person who proves you can turn anything into something unforgettable if you show up fully. Which is a lot like cooking, honestly.

Sometimes, you're the main dish—big and shiny and everyone's excited. Sometimes, you're the side—quietly holding the whole plate together. But if you do it with excellence? If you bring the flavor? If you show up like it matters? People remember. So, in honor of our Thursday-night theater pilgrimages . . . and in honor of Kayla, the most iconic body of water to ever grace a stage . . . Let's make my favorite half-priced appetizer at home.

Because this Slow Cooker Spinach & Artichoke Dip is the kind of warm, cheesy comfort that makes you want to laugh in a restaurant booth with your best friends and talk about the good old days like you never left them. And baby, we're doing it with our whole selves.

# Slow Cooker Spinach & Artichoke Dip

SERVES 10 TO 12 *(as an appetizer)*

**prep:** 10 minutes | **cook:** 2 hours | **total:** 2 hours 10 minutes

*"Healthy," in the same way a casserole is a "vegetable"—there's spinach in it, and that's the testimony. This dip has spinach and artichokes, which means it's basically a salad . . . if you like your salad warm, creamy, and emotionally supportive. Stir it up, plug it in, and grab a cracker. Let's live.*

- **1 (10-ounce) package frozen chopped spinach**
- **2 (14-ounce) cans quartered artichoke hearts, drained and roughly chopped**
- **1 cup white wine (Pinot Grigio works great)**
- **1 cup sour cream**
- **¾ cup freshly grated Parmesan cheese**
- **½ cup crumbled feta cheese**
- **⅓ cup mayonnaise**
- **2 tablespoons garlic powder**
- **1 tablespoon onion powder**
- **1 cracklin' of black pepper (or ¼ teaspoon, if you're being "measured")**
- **8 ounces cream cheese,* cut into cubes or left as a block**
- **Pita bread, to serve**

**1. Prep the spinach like you mean it.** Thaw the spinach and squeeze it dry—and then squeeze it again. If your spinach is still weeping, your dip will, too.

**2. Mix it up.** In a large bowl, combine the artichokes, white wine, sour cream, Parmesan, feta, mayonnaise, garlic powder, onion powder, black pepper, and spinach. Stir until everything is well combined.

**3. Into the slow cooker.** Spoon the mixture into your slow cooker and spread it out evenly.

**4. Add the cream cheese last.** Place the cream cheese on top (block or cubes). Cover.

**5. Cook.** Cook on high for 2 hours, stirring once or twice as it melts and becomes the creamy dream it was born to be.

**6. Stir and serve.** Give it a final stir, taste for seasoning, and serve hot with pita bread, or whatever you've got that can scoop.

**We used Philadelphia Cream Cheese.*

## Kitchen Tips

- Squeeze the spinach dry. I'm saying it AGAIN because this is where people lose the plot.
- Freshly grate your Parmesan if you can. It melts smoother and tastes richer.
- Want it extra cozy? Add another 2 to 4 ounces of cream cheese. I won't tell.
- Make it like Luci: Add a few dashes of hot sauce or a pinch of red pepper flakes.
- Make Ahead: Mix everything (except cream cheese) up to 24 hours in advance, and refrigerate. When ready, add to slow cooker, and top with cream cheese.
- Storage: Refrigerate leftovers in an airtight container for 3 to 4 days.
- Reheat: Warm in the microwave in 30-second bursts, stirring in between, or reheat on LOW in the slow cooker until hot. Add a splash of milk or cream if it thickens too much.

warm
high

# Peek Before You Leap

Dianna and I had no business pushing a full-sized rowboat around the edge of the theater stage while belting "Kiss the Girl" in a college production of *The Little Mermaid*, especially not in head-to-toe sea creature costumes.

Not because we couldn't sing—please. We had been leads in our college glory days. We knew how to hit a note, hold a harmony, and cry prettily into a spotlight like it was our spiritual gift. The problem wasn't talent.

The problem was *liability*. Because at the end of the day, no amount of vocal training prepares you for this: two fully grown human beings sitting in a rowboat while you and your best friend—dressed like aquatic nonsense—try to scoot said boat around a stage ledge that's about as wide as a Communion wafer.

That stage edge was tiny. A decorative trim. A sliver. The kind of edge that looks harmless until you realize you're responsible for steering a boat that holds two living, breathing human beings inside of it.

Now, let me back up. Dianna and I decided to audition for *The Little Mermaid* at our local college because we missed theater. We missed how fun it was onstage—how your problems are small enough to solve with hairspray and a prayer. And more than anything, we missed our favorite director in the world: Mr. Sirmon.

Mr. Sirmon is the kind of director who can make you feel like you're capable of performing on Broadway . . . even if you're standing there in borrowed character shoes and an emotional support bobby pin. He has vision. He has standards. He has that sparkle in his eye that says, *I can make this magical*, even when the budget says, *You can make this . . . creative.*

We weren't there to reclaim the spotlight. We were there for joy. For moral support. For the thrill of being back in the room where people speak fluent chaos and call it "blocking."

And sure enough—Dianna and I got cast as Ariel's older sisters, Aquata and Andrina. We were also double-cast as sea creatures for the "Under the Sea" and "Kiss the Girl" numbers, which is theater code for: We trust you with harmonies and rhinestones, but we will not be handing you anything that requires a waiver. Joke's on all of us.

Because the set was stunning. Truly. There was a rake built in—meaning the back of the stage was elevated like a gentle hill—so the undersea world looked deep and dreamy, like you were staring into an aquarium designed by someone with both artistic vision and a suspiciously large donation.

Our costumes were custom-made for our figures—bless the costume shop saints who took one look at us and said, "We will not shame you. We will support you. We will lift, tuck, and sparkle you into dignity."

At one point, Mr. Sirmon got excited—because directors are always excited right before they try to end your life—and announced we would be wearing roller skates to create a steady flow onstage. To emulate swimming under the sea. Roller skates. On a rake. In the dark. While singing. In corsets.

Dianna and I looked at each other like, *If this man puts wheels on my feet, I will meet Jesus in the wings.* Mercifully, that idea died a quick and quiet death after Mr. Sirmon watched us attempt to walk up the rake on our own two feet, without skates, and he realized we were moving less like mermaids and more like newborn giraffes learning the concept of gravity.

Still, we rehearsed hard. 12 hours a week. We knew the show. We knew every cue, every harmony, every "don't stand there or you'll get decapitated by a swinging seaweed set piece" moment. But before we get to my personal humiliation . . . we need to talk about the rowboat. Because the rowboat was Dianna's villain origin story.

There we were in full costume—sparkling, sweating, serving "under the sea" fantasy—when we got assigned the task of pushing a full-sized rowboat around the edge of the stage. A boat. On an edge. With two human beings inside it.

Dianna saw the danger immediately, because Dianna is the kind of person whose brain comes with a built-in risk-assessment department. She was looking at that ledge like an actuary at a trampoline park. Two inches to the right, and those two precious souls in the rowboat were going straight into the orchestra pit. And if you've never seen a trombone player confronted by an incoming boat, let me tell you—nobody has the emotional training for that.

Two inches to the left, and the whole boat would've capsized into the audience like a show nobody consented to attend. And what was I doing? Performing. Working the crowd. Smiling at people like I was the captain of the boat myself. We'll call it the USS *Confidence*.

Because here's something I have learned about myself: When I'm nervous, I get theatrical. It's my coping mechanism. Some people go quiet. Some people get serious. I start serving facial expressions like I'm paid by the eyebrow flex. So, I'm out there acting like everything is fine—singing, sparkling, waving, engaging the front row like we are not one wrong nudge away from a maritime tragedy.

Meanwhile, Dianna is facing me from the bow of the boat, having what can only be described as a full-body panic attack wrapped in a seashell wig, while I'm at the stern of the boat throwing a party.

She was pulling that boat like she was defusing a bomb. Her eyes were wide. Her jaw was clenched. Her shoulders were up around her ears. She had the kind of expression you see on women who have just realized they are the only adult in the situation.

At one point she hissed through her teeth, still smiling for the audience, "MEGHAN." And I hissed back, still smiling, "YES?"

And she said, "WE ARE GOING TO KILL SOMEONE."

And I said, "WE GOT THIS." Because the audience doesn't need to know we're seconds away from becoming a news headline: LOCAL WOMEN IN SEA CREATURE COSTUMES LAUNCH BOAT INTO ORCHESTRA PIT.

So, every night of the performance, Dianna pulled that rowboat with the precision of a surgeon, while I acted like we were gliding gracefully through the ocean. She was doing geometry. I was doing jazz hands.

And I swear to you, the boat itself could sense the tension. It creaked. It wobbled. It leaned. It flirted with disaster like it was trying to get cast as Ursula.

Dianna's panic became a regular part of the show. She'd pull, and I'd beam. She'd white-knuckle the edge, and I'd wink at somebody's Mamaw in the third row like, *Yes ma'am, this is my calling.*

She'd whisper prayers under her breath, and I'd sing harmony like I wasn't living on the edge—literally and spiritually. And we survived. Night after night. We kept the boat out of the orchestra. We kept the boat out of the audience. We kept the boat from becoming a lawsuit.

But you know what it taught me? It taught me the most important kind of partnership is not the kind where both people do the same thing. It's the kind where one person keeps you joyful and the other person keeps you alive. And that's not just theater. That's life. That's marriage. That's friendship. That's motherhood. That's the kitchen. Because the kitchen has its own version of the stage edge. One inch too far, and you're cutting toward your palm. Two seconds too long, and your shrimp go from tender to tragic.

One distracted moment, and your butter turns to blackened carbon. And the truth is: Most disasters don't come from big dramatic choices. They come from tiny margins. A little too fast. A little too confident. A little too "I've done this a hundred times." That's how you end up burning the garlic. Over-salting the sauce. Forgetting the timer.

Pushing the boat while smiling at the audience. Sometimes, the most loving thing you can do—for your people and for yourself—is to slow down and respect the edge. Let the cautious friend be cautious. Let the responsible voice in your head speak up. And for the love of all things holy, don't try to balance a whole lot of moving parts without first looking at where your feet are.

Which brings me to the night my feet betrayed me. We had a quick change in this show. Oh, the quick change.

Dianna and I had to go from ridiculous sea creatures—huge wigs, seashells piled on our heads like Neptune's Pinterest board—back into mermaid looks in less than 45 seconds.

That means we had 45 seconds to:

1. Exit the stage
2. Become a different species
3. Re-lace into a corset that squeezed us like it had personal beef with our lungs
4. Return to the stage smiling like we weren't being actively compressed by said corset.

To get offstage fast enough, I had a shortcut: Midway up the rake, I'd leap off the side of the stage into complete darkness and run to the back hallway like I was escaping consequences. I had done it multiple times a night. Every night. I knew that leap. I trusted that leap. That leap and I were in a committed relationship. We were deep into a dress rehearsal, nearing the end of "Kiss the Girl," hitting those last harmonies like we were paid professionals and not two women with shell wigs and cortisol levels through the roof.

The song ended. The applause was imaginary. The adrenaline was real. I turned and ran for my quick change like I always did. In my mind, I was a gazelle. In reality, I was a woman in a rhinestoned sea creature costume trying to outrun time.

I reached my spot and launched myself into the darkness with full confidence—arms ready, spirit willing, ankles uncertain. And that's when I met . . . the boulder. A prop boulder, nearly my height, sitting offstage in the wings like it owned the building. Nobody told us it had been moved there. Nobody warned me. It was placed perfectly out of my line of sight—like a trap designed by someone who hates joy.

My back foot clipped it. And friends . . . physics took over. One second, I was leaping. The next second, I was airborne. Arms spread like an eagle. Legs over my head. I did not so much "fall" as I performed a full-body surrender to humiliation.

I belly flopped and slid across the floor. And the rhinestones—those beautiful, shiny little demons—stabbed into my skin like tiny sparkling daggers. I felt the scrape. I felt the sting. I felt my soul leave my body briefly and hover above the scene like, *Girl . . . is this your testimony?* I laid there in the darkness bruised, bleeding, and mortified. My pride, however, was the real casualty. Because here's the thing about theater: There is always someone watching, even when you think you're hidden. I could hear the gasp from the crew. I could feel the shift in energy. And I could practically sense Dianna's eyes widening somewhere nearby like, *Lord, she is down. She is DOWN down.* But the show doesn't stop for your dignity. The show doesn't pause for your bruises.

And it certainly doesn't care about your ego. So, I peeled myself off the floor like a sticker that had lost its will to live, sprinted to the back hallway, and completed the quickest quick change of my life while silently cussing that boulder in the name of the Father, Son, and Holy Spirit.

And then—because theater is an illness—we walked back onstage moments later, corseted, sparkling, smiling. As if I hadn't just fought a rock and lost.

Later, I inspected the bruises and puncture wounds and thought, *Well. That'll look cute tomorrow.* But as I sat there, still shaken, I realized something: That boulder didn't just trip my foot. It tripped my assumption.

I assumed the path would always be clear because it had been clear before. I assumed someone would warn me if something changed. I assumed I could move full speed through the dark and nothing would be in my way.

And bless it—that's exactly how we cook sometimes. We rush. We assume. We go on autopilot. We think, *I've done this before. I don't need to check. I don't need to slow down.* And then we grab the hot pan without an oven mitt. Or we forget the shrimp in the skillet because we're answering a text. Or we assume the knife is in its "usual place" and discover it isn't—with our fingertips.

Sometimes, we don't get hurt because we don't know what we're doing. Sometimes, we get hurt because we think we know it so well we stop paying attention. The lesson isn't "be afraid." The lesson is: Slow down long enough to look. Do a quick peek before you leap.

Before you toss seafood in the pan, make sure everything is ready—because shrimp waits on no one. Fish goes from tender to tough in half a minute. And crab cakes do not care that your child has appeared beside you holding a snack while asking for a snack.

Cooking is like theater: The timing matters, the preparation matters, and the moments that feel chaotic are usually the ones where you need to breathe and take your cues. And if someone puts a boulder in your way—onstage or in life—just know this: You can still get back up, fix your wig, and hit your mark. Also—if you ever find yourself pushing a boat around a tiny ledge in the dark, smiling at the audience while your best friend is having a panic attack . . . listen to Dianna. She is the reason everybody lived. So anyway . . . here's a collection of seafood recipes in honor of the cast members who didn't warn me about the boulder in the wings that night. Amen.

# Shrimp Scampi Dip

**SERVES 6 TO 8** *(or 3 to 4 if your friends "just want a bite" 37 times)*

**prep:** 15 minutes | **cook:** 20 minutes | **total:** 35 minutes

*This dip is basically shrimp scampi that decided it wanted to be the center of attention. It's buttery, garlicky, lemony, a little wine-kissed, and baked until it's bubbling like it has gossip to share. Serve it with chips and watch grown adults become feral.*

- **2 tablespoons unsalted butter**
- **8 ounces fresh medium Gulf shrimp, peeled and deveined, chopped**
- **2 teaspoons garlic powder**
- **¼ teaspoon ground black pepper**
- **¼ cup dry white wine (Pinot Grigio works great)**
- **2 tablespoons fresh lemon juice**
- **¾ cup freshly grated Parmesan cheese, plus extra for topping**
- **¼ cup sour cream**
- **4 ounces cream cheese, softened**
- **3 tablespoons mayonnaise**

**1. Preheat and grease.** Preheat your oven to 350°. Lightly spray a small baking dish with cooking spray.

**2. Cook the shrimp.** In a large skillet, melt the butter over medium heat. Add the chopped shrimp, garlic powder, and black pepper. Cook, stirring until shrimp are pink and just cooked through, about 3 to 4 minutes. Pour in the white wine and lemon juice, stirring for about 30 seconds to wake up all that flavor.

**3. Make it saucy.** Turn off the heat. Add the Parmesan, sour cream, cream cheese, and mayonnaise. Stir until everything is melty, creamy, and fully combined. Transfer the dip to your prepared baking dish. Sprinkle extra Parmesan over the top.

**4. Bake and serve.** Bake until hot and bubbling, 15 minutes. Increase oven temperature to broil, and broil just until the top is golden and bubbly, 3 to 4 minutes. Stay close. Broilers don't cook—they ambush.

# Gulf Coast Chowder with Puff Pastry Sticks for Dippin'

SERVES 8 TO 10

**prep:** 25 minutes | **cook:** 40 minutes | **total:** 1 hour 5 minutes

*This chowder tastes like the Gulf Coast hugged you, patted your cheek, and said, "Baby, sit down. You look tired." It's got shrimp, sausage, lump crab, sweet corn, tender potatoes, and a savory broth that makes people hover near the stove like they're waiting on a concert encore. And yes—Puff Pastry Sticks for dippin'.*

- 1 tablespoon olive oil (plus a drizzle more if needed)
- 1 pound fresh medium Gulf shrimp, peeled and deveined
- 1 pound smoked sausage, sliced or diced
- ¼ cup salted butter
- 1 large Vidalia onion, diced
- 2½ cups yellow corn
- 1 tablespoon Old Bay seasoning, plus more for garnish
- ½ teaspoon Creole seasoning
- 1 teaspoon garlic powder
- 1 teaspoon onion powder
- Dash of salt
- Cracklin' of black pepper
- 1½ cups dry white wine (Pinot Grigio is great)
- ½ cup all-purpose flour
- 3 cups seafood stock
- 1 pound Yukon gold potatoes, peeled and diced
- 3 to 4 bay leaves
- 1 tablespoon chopped fresh thyme (or 1 teaspoon dried)
- 1 lemon (see lemon trick in Step 6 below)
- 1 pound lump crabmeat (picked through for shells—because surprise shell bits are not the vibe)
- 1 cup heavy cream
- Puff Pastry Sticks, to serve

**1. Sear the shrimp and sausage.** In a large heavy pot or Dutch oven, heat olive oil over medium-high heat. Add the shrimp and sausage, and sauté until the shrimp are just pink, about 2 to 3 minutes. Remove shrimp and sausage to a plate. (We'll bring them back later—nobody overcooks shrimp on my watch.)

**2. Build the base.** In the same pot, melt the butter. Sauté the onion over medium-low heat until soft and translucent, about 4 to 5 minutes. Add the corn, and stir.

**3. Season it like you mean it.** Add Old Bay, Creole seasoning, garlic powder, onion powder, salt, pepper, and stir until everything smells like you're doing something important.

**4. Deglaze and reduce.** Pour in the white wine. Bring to a simmer, and let it cook until reduced by about half, 6 to 7 minutes.

**5. Make your roux moment.** Sprinkle in the flour, and whisk or stir constantly until smooth and thickened, about 1 to 2 minutes.

**6. Add stock and simmer.** Slowly pour in the seafood stock, stirring as you go to keep it lump-free. Add the potatoes, bay leaves, thyme, and the lemon. Lemon trick: You can add it whole, pierced a few times with a knife, or add thick slices. It perfumes the chowder without making it sour.

**7. Cook until potatoes are tender.** Simmer, uncovered, for about 25 minutes, stirring occasionally, until potatoes are fork-tender.

**8. Finish the chowder.** Remove and discard the lemon and bay leaves. Stir in the crab, then return the shrimp and sausage to the pot. Pour in the heavy cream, and gently stir until warmed through, 2 to 3 minutes. Garnish with Old Bay, and serve hot with Puff Pastry Sticks for dippin'—because chowder deserves accessories.

# Puff Pastry Sticks

**SERVES 8 TO 10**

**prep:** 10 minutes
**cook:** 12 to 15 minutes
**total:** 22 to 25 minutes

*These are the crunchy little sidekicks your chowder deserves—golden, flaky, and dangerously snackable. They look fancy, but they're basically just puff pastry in a cute outfit.*

- 1 **(17.3-ounce) box frozen puff pastry, thawed according to package directions**
- 1 **large egg (for egg wash)**
- 1 **tablespoon water**
- ¼ **teaspoon salt**
- ½ **teaspoon garlic powder (optional, but encouraged)**
- ½ **teaspoon smoked paprika (optional)**
- ¼ **cup freshly grated Parmesan cheese (optional, but makes them feel "restaurant")**
- **Ground black pepper (optional, but she's pretty)**

**1. Preheat and prep.** Preheat your oven to 400°. Line a large baking sheet with parchment paper.
**2. Shape sticks.** Lightly flour your counter and gently roll each puff pastry sheet just enough to smooth it out.
**3. Egg wash magic.** Whisk together egg and 1 tablespoon water. Brush egg wash over the surface of the pastry. Sprinkle with salt, garlic powder, smoked paprika, Parmesan, and pepper, if using.
**4. Slice into sticks.** Using a pizza cutter or sharp knife, cut into strips—about ½ to ¾ inch wide. Twist each strip a few times, and place on the prepared baking sheet, leaving a little space between them.
**5. Bake them up.** Bake 12 to 15 minutes until puffed and deeply golden. Let cool 3 to 5 minutes, and serve warm beside your chowder.

4

# Casseroles & Comfort Food

This chapter is where comfort pulls up a chair and stays a while. Casseroles are a Southern love letter. They say, "I'm sorry you're hurting," "Congratulations," and "I don't know what else to do, so I brought something good." Around here, comfort food is not just food—it is communication with a topping. It's about the kind of comfort that reaches past your appetite and settles somewhere deeper. The kind of comfort that reminds you you're not alone, even on the days life feels too heavy to carry gracefully.

# The Turkey's Last Flight

In my family, holidays are not merely dates on a calendar. They are full-blown theatrical productions on both sides. Thanksgiving, in particular, is the feast of all feasts. The dining table becomes a culinary landscape, a smorgasbord of biblical proportions. Casseroles steam, gravies glisten, and an assortment of pies perfume the air around us. Mawmaw, the culinary queen, pours her heart and soul into every dish, creating a spread so magnificent you'd think she was preparing to feed the 5,000 instead of just 20 or so hungry family members. Food is our love language, a way for us to make love tangible, and by that measure, Mawmaw could feed a small nation.

Now, every Thanksgiving, the pièce de résistance is the turkey—a golden-brown masterpiece that Mawmaw has seasoned and roasted to perfection. And the honor of transporting this titan of poultry from the oven to the carving station falls on one man: my Pawpaw. Pawpaw is a man who moves through life with a never-ending chuckle bubbling just beneath the surface. He is the maestro of mischief, possessing a childlike wonder that is both his greatest charm and also his greatest liability. On this particular Thanksgiving, that liability was about to take center stage.

Pawpaw armed himself with two oven mitts and a grin that stretched from ear to ear. He opened the oven door and slid the massive roasting pan out as if it were the grand prize on a game show. "Behold!" he announced, his laughter echoing through the kitchen. But that childlike wonder can be a slippery slope—especially when you're balancing a steaming hot 24-pound turkey in your hands.

And then, in a perfect storm of both haste and humor, Pawpaw's left foot got tangled up with his right foot. Time seemed to slow down. He tripped—oh yes, he tripped—and in a scene that could've been pulled straight from a cartoon, that turkey launched into its last flight. The turkey, loosed from its earthly bonds, took to the air. It was a brief but majestic arc, a poultry projectile soaring over the kitchen island before landing with a resounding thud on the linoleum floor. Propelled by its own momentum, it slid another 3 feet before stopping while the rest of us stood in shock.

We all stood in stunned silence, mouths open wide, processing the gravity of the situation. I metaphorically clutched my pearls. Mawmaw, her patience worn thin from hours upon hours of orchestrating this culinary marathon, slowly turned her head. The look she gave Pawpaw was a quiet, controlled fury, the look of a woman who has seen too much. Her glare could have curdled milk. "Pick up the bird, Roland," she hissed through gritted teeth, her hands on her hips. Her voice was dangerously even, each word clipped and precise.

It wasn't a suggestion. It was a commandment. Pawpaw—still wearing his oven mitts like boxing gloves—looked at the turkey, then at Mawmaw, and then did the most Pawpaw thing imaginable. He shrugged. And chuckled. "It'll be fine!" he said, like this was a minor inconvenience and not a culinary felony. "I'm sure it'll taste just the same!" Now, I should've been horrified. I should've been stunned into silence. But something in me snapped—not my sanity, just my restraint—and I erupted into giggles. I tried to stop. I truly did.

But the sight of that bird performing its final, undignified ballet was too much. There is something deeply absurd about a turkey sliding across the floor like a slapstick prop in a low-budget comedy. It was humiliating. It was dramatic. It was—if we're being honest—kind of iconic.

And that's how, my friends, we ate turkey off the floor. Now, before you call the health department, I need you to understand: Mawmaw cleaned it. The turkey was . . . *addressed*. There was a solid amount of "cut that part off" and "Lord forgive us" and "Lord please bless this food."

We sat down to eat with a bird that had taken an adventurous tumble and a family that couldn't stop laughing. And just when you think Pawpaw would let the moment die, he had to add one more line—because he is incapable of leaving well enough alone.

He leaned back in his chair, looked around the table with that mischievous glimmer in his eye, and said: "Well now . . . I guess we'll have *ground* turkey instead of sliced!"

His laughter rang out like jingle bells, and even Mawmaw's mouth twitched—just slightly—like her face wanted to laugh but her principles said no. And that's the thing about family meals, isn't it? The food matters. But it's never been the whole point. The meal is the backdrop. The real feast is the love. The laughter. The stories that get told every year until they become legend. The reminders that perfection was never the invitation—*presence* was.

And if we're honest, that turkey taught me something that still applies in every kitchen I step into: You can plan. You can prep. You can season and roast and do everything "right" . . . and life can still trip you up right at the finish line. But a mishap doesn't have to ruin the moment. Sometimes, it becomes the moment.

So, if your casserole looks questionable, if your rolls are more "hard" than "homemade," if your ham is dry, and your aunt is emotionally hydrated (aka crying), and the dog just stole something off the counter—breathe. Laugh. Cut around the rough parts. And keep serving love. Because people won't remember if the turkey was perfect.

They'll remember how it felt to be at your table. So with that spirit—of comfort, joy, and a healthy respect for gravity—let's move into my favorite holiday recipes. The casseroles that show up faithfully every year. The dishes that make grown people act unsupervised. The kind of food that tastes like home, even when your home is loud, chaotic, and occasionally hosting a turkey that's been on the floor. Roll up your sleeves, honey. And maybe—just maybe—watch your step.

# Parmesan Butternut Squash Casserole

SERVES 6 TO 8

**prep:** 20 minutes | **cook:** 45 minutes | **total:** 1 hour 10 minutes *(includes rest time)*

*This casserole is confusing—in the best way. Because it's just butternut squash, onion, Parmesan, breadcrumbs . . . and then, out of nowhere, a dollop of mayo comes sliding in like, "Don't worry, I'm still Southern." Somehow, it tastes elevated anyway. It's the rare dish that can sit on a holiday table and please both the food snobs and the folks who think vegetables are a suggestion.*

**Softened butter, for the baking dish**
**3 cups butternut squash, peeled and cut into ¾-inch chunks**
**2 tablespoons salted butter**
**1 cup finely chopped sweet onion**
**1 large egg**
**2 tablespoons mayonnaise**
**Salt and ground black pepper, to taste**
**⅔ cup freshly shredded Parmesan cheese, divided**
**⅓ cup Italian-style breadcrumbs**

**1. Preheat and grease.** Preheat your oven to 350°. Butter an 8x8-inch baking dish (or similar size).
**2. Cook the squash.** Bring a pot of salted water to a boil. Add the butternut squash, and cook until fork-tender, about 15 minutes. Drain well.
**3. Sauté the onion.** While the squash cooks, in a medium skillet, melt butter over medium heat. Add chopped onion, and sauté until soft and translucent, about 4 to 6 minutes.
**4. Mix the base.** In a large bowl, beat the egg. Whisk in mayonnaise, then season with a pinch of salt and a cracklin' of pepper.
**5. Add the good stuff.** Stir in ⅓ cup Parmesan and the Italian-style breadcrumbs. (The breadcrumbs bring their own seasoning to the party, which we appreciate.)
**6. Fold it together.** Add the sautéed onion and drained squash. Gently fold until everything is evenly coated.
**7. Bake.** Spread the mixture into the prepared dish. Sprinkle the remaining ⅓ cup Parmesan evenly over the top. Bake until set and golden brown on top, about 45 minutes. Let rest 5 to 10 minutes before serving.

## Kitchen Tips

* Drain the squash well. Excess water is the enemy of a good casserole. Let it sit in the colander for 1 to 2 minutes if needed.
* If you want a slightly smoother texture, lightly mash a portion of the squash before mixing—but don't turn it into baby food.
* For extra browning, pop it under the broiler for 1 to 2 minutes at the end (watch closely).
* This is one of those dishes that tastes even better when it's had a minute to cool and settle. Like people.
* Make Ahead: Assemble the casserole (up to the Parmesan topping), cover, and refrigerate up to 24 hours. Bake as directed, adding 5 to 10 minutes if baking straight from the fridge.
* Storage: Refrigerate leftovers covered for 3 to 4 days.
* Reheat: Warm in a 350° oven until heated through, or microwave individual portions. Add a tiny sprinkle of Parmesan on top if you want to revive the glam.

# Mawmaw's Dressing

SERVES 10 TO 12

**prep:** 25 minutes *(plus cooling cornbread)* | **cook:** 35 to 45 minutes | **total:** 1 hour 10 minutes *(plus resting)*

*Mawmaw's Dressing isn't just a side dish—it's a timeline. It tastes like every Thanksgiving I've ever known, like paper plates stacked too high, laughter from the next room, and the kind of comfort you don't realize you're memorizing until years later when you're standing in your own kitchen trying to make it taste the same.*

**3 (8.5-ounce) boxes cornbread mix***
**5 slices white bread**
**A little salted butter or a splash of broth**
**1 medium onion, chopped small**
**3 to 4 stalks celery, chopped small**
**Softened butter, for the baking dish**
**2 tablespoons chopped fresh sage**
**Salt and ground black pepper, to taste**
**3 to 4 cups chicken broth (plus more if needed)**
**Garnish: whole fresh sage leaves**

**1. Bake the cornbread.** Prepare and bake all 3 boxes of cornbread mix according to the package directions. Let the cornbread cool completely, and crumble it into a big mixing bowl.

**2. Toast the bread.** Toast bread until golden, and chop into small pieces. Add to the bowl with the cornbread.

**3. Cook the "good smell" vegetables.** In a medium skillet, add a little butter or a splash of broth, the chopped onion, and celery; sauté over medium heat until softened, about 6 to 8 minutes. Add vegetables to the cornbread mixture.

**4. Preheat and grease.** Preheat your oven to 350°. Grease a 9x13-inch baking dish with butter.

**5. Season like Mawmaw.** Add the sage to the cornbread mixture, and season with salt and pepper. (Go easy on salt until the broth goes in.)

**6. Add broth until it looks right.** Pour in 3 cups chicken broth to start, mixing gently. Add more broth as needed until the mixture is very moist—like thick oatmeal. You want it soft and scoopable, not dry and crumbly. Spread the mixture evenly into the prepared dish. If you're making your own broth, strain it and use it the same way.

**7. Bake it just right.** Bake until the top is lightly golden and the center is set but still moist, 35 to 45 minutes. Let it sit for 10 minutes. Garnish with fresh sage and serve.

**I use Jiffy cornbread mix.*

## Kitchen Tips

* Moisture is everything. Dressing dries out fast, so err on the side of wetter before baking.
* Taste your broth first. Some broths are salty enough to do all the seasoning for you.
* Want it richer? Add a few tablespoons of melted butter over the top before baking. Mawmaw wouldn't be mad about it.
* Make Ahead: Assemble the dressing (without baking) up to 24 hours ahead. Cover and refrigerate. Add a splash of broth before baking if it looks dry.
* Storage: Refrigerate leftovers in an airtight container for up to 4 days.
* Reheat: Cover with foil and warm at 325° until heated through, adding a splash of broth if needed.

# White Cheddar Green Bean Casserole

SERVES 10 TO 12

**prep:** 15 minutes | **cook:** 25 minutes | **total:** 40 minutes

*Green bean casserole is already a Thanksgiving celebrity, but this version shows up in a white Cheddar gown with crispy bacon as her date. It's creamy, it's cheesy, and it's topped with those crispy fried onions we all "buy for the casserole" but end up snacking on all the whole way home from the grocery store.*

- **1 (12-ounce) package center-cut bacon, chopped**
- **1 yellow onion, diced**
- **3 tablespoons unsalted butter**
- **3 tablespoons all-purpose flour**
- **1½ cups whole milk**
- **½ teaspoon garlic powder (or "a little bit")**
- **½ teaspoon kosher salt**
- **¼ teaspoon ground black pepper (a good cracklin')**
- **1 cup freshly shredded extra-sharp white Cheddar cheese**
- **3 (14.5-ounce) cans green beans, drained well**
- **1 (6-ounce) container crispy fried onions**

**1. Preheat and grease.** Preheat your oven to 350°. Lightly spray a 13x9-inch baking dish with cooking spray.

**2. Cook the bacon.** In a large skillet, cook chopped bacon over medium heat until crisp. Transfer bacon to a paper towel–lined plate, but leave about 2 tablespoons drippings in the skillet (that's flavor, baby).

**3. Sauté the onion.** Add onion to the bacon drippings. Cook until softened and translucent, 4 to 5 minutes.

**4. Make the roux.** Add butter to the skillet. Once melted, whisk in the flour, and cook 1 minute to get rid of that raw flour taste.

**5. Make it creamy.** Slowly whisk in the milk, stirring constantly, and cook until smooth and thickened, 2 to 4 minutes.

**6. Season and cheese.** Stir in garlic powder, salt, and pepper. Add shredded white Cheddar, and stir until melted and silky.

**7. Bring it together.** Stir in the cooked bacon and drained green beans until everything is coated in the sauce. Pour mixture into the prepared dish, and spread evenly. Top with crispy fried onions.

**8. Bake.** Bake for 25 minutes until hot and bubbly and the onions are golden.

## Kitchen Tips

- Drain those green beans well or your casserole will be soupy and sad.
- Freshly shredded cheese melts better than preshredded (which has anti-caking agents that make sauces less smooth).
- Want it extra luxe? Add an extra ½ cup Cheddar, because cheese is never the problem.
- If your fried onions brown too fast, loosely tent with foil for the last 10 minutes.
- Make Ahead: Assemble the casserole without the fried onions, cover, and refrigerate up to 24 hours. Add onions right before baking.
- Storage: Refrigerate leftovers covered in the fridge for 3 to 4 days.
- Reheat: Warm in a 350° oven until heated through. If you want the top crispy again, add a fresh handful of fried onions during the last 5 minutes.

# Motherhood: The Recipe I Didn't Write

Let me tell y'all something: I have made some incredible things in my kitchen. I have browned butter until it smells like pure magic. I have pulled casseroles out of the oven so bubbly they look like they're putting on a performance. I have watched people take one bite of a recipe and get quiet—because you know it's good when the whole room goes silent. But I have never made anything as miraculous as my children.

I'm a mother of two, and I will never get over it. I don't care how many times it happens across the earth, every day, for all of human history—bringing a child into the world is still the wildest thing I've ever witnessed up close. The fact that two whole humans live in my house and call me "Mama"?—That's absolutely incredible. And what gets me is the math of it all.

For my little boy and my little girl to exist, everything had to line up perfectly—generation after generation after generation. A thousand tiny decisions that felt ordinary at the time. One person moving, or not moving. One conversation. One "what if." And somehow—through wars and weather and heartbreak and detours and answered prayers and the kind of timing you can't explain—here we are. Two kids who are 17 months apart. Which is close enough that some days it feels like I blinked and suddenly I had a full-sized family.

Now listen—I'm an only child. I didn't grow up with siblings. I didn't have a built-in best friend who also steals your snacks and then swears on everything holy that they didn't. I knew cousins. I knew chosen family. But the sibling thing? I didn't get it. I didn't have it. And then I had my son. And then, just when I thought my heart couldn't stretch any wider—here came my daughter.

And suddenly, I'm watching the sibling dynamic unfold in real time like it's a documentary I didn't know I needed. Some days, they are precious. They're tender. They're curled up on the couch together like little peas in a pod. And other days? One of them is breathing the wrong way and the other one is ready to call the authorities. But even in the chaos—especially in the chaos—it's beautiful.

Because I'm watching them learn how to share and how to forgive. How to be brave. How to be gentle. How to be themselves while still belonging to each other. I'm watching them build a bond I didn't get to experience as a kid—and it feels like God is letting me peek into a kind of love I didn't know firsthand until now.

And I'm proud of them. I'm proud of my boy—his mind, his humor, his tenderness, the way he's growing into himself. And I'm proud of my girl—her fire, her sweetness, the way she takes up space like she was born knowing she belongs here. And genetics? Don't even get me started.

Because you'll look at your child and realize: Oh. That is my daddy's analytical mind. Or, that attitude right

there is mine, and I'd like to apologize to my own mother publicly. It's like the Lord reached into two entire family histories, shook them up like a snow globe, and said, "Here. Watch this."

And I know motherhood is hard. It is the hardest, holiest work I've ever done. It will exhaust you, expose you, and sanctify you—sometimes all before breakfast.

But it's also a miracle I get to live inside. Because it's not just that I have children. It's that I get to witness them. To watch their personalities unfold. To see the moment they learn something new. To hear them laugh like joy is brand new. To comfort them when the world disappoints them. To teach them what love looks like when it's steady, and patient, and present.

And yes—I believe God did the miracle. But I also believe He let me help. That's what motherhood feels like to me: partnering with heaven in the most humbling way. Being trusted with souls. Being handed the responsibility of building a home that feels safe. And if you're wondering how this ties into cooking, I'll tell you.

Because food is one of the first ways we learn love. It's the snack cut into triangles because triangles taste better, obviously. It's the extra scoop because "you're growing." It's the comfort meal when somebody had a rough day. It's the birthday cake with crooked candles and everybody singing too loud. It's the table where we gather, even when we're tired. It's the kitchen where we learn that nourishment is more than calories—it's care.

Motherhood is a recipe you don't write down. You just make it, every day. With what you've got. With patience when you can find it. With humor when you're hanging by a thread. With prayer when you don't know what else to do.

And if I've learned anything, it's this: The most important thing I'll ever make in this life isn't a casserole. It's a home. A steady place. A table. A love that keeps showing up. And I'm grateful—deep in my bones grateful—that I get to be their mama.

In my house, my children's favorite food isn't fancy. It's not photogenic. It's not going to win a beauty pageant. But it is comfort in a slow cooker. It's the meal they request when they've had a big day. The smell that makes them wander into the kitchen like hungry little bears. The kind of dish that turns everyone softer around the table. Chicken thighs. Cream cheese. A good heaping spoonful of ranch seasoning. That's it.

And somehow, those three humble ingredients turn into the kind of comfort food that makes your whole house feel like it's exhaling.

So, in honor of motherhood—of full hearts, busy nights, and little voices saying, "Mama, can we have Comfort Chicken again?"—On the next page is the recipe that my kids request more than anything else.

# Comfort Chicken

SERVES 4 TO 6

**prep:** 5 minutes | **cook:** 4 to 6 hours (LOW) or 2 to 3 hours (HIGH) | **total:** 3 to 8 hours *(depending on cook time)*

*My children light up when they smell this chicken in the slow cooker. This is one of those recipes that feels like a warm blanket with a side of "everybody hush and eat." And if you're feeding picky people, tired people, or tiny people who live on vibes and ranch seasoning—this one's for you.*

**1 package boneless, skinless chicken thighs (about 2 to 2½ pounds)**
**2 heaping teaspoons ranch seasoning mix**
**1 (8-ounce) block cream cheese***
**Buns, rice, baked potatoes, or toasted bread, to serve (optional but highly encouraged)**

***I use Philadelphia cream cheese.***

**1. Load the slow cooker.** Add the chicken thighs to a slow cooker in an even layer.

**2. Season.** Sprinkle the ranch seasoning evenly over the chicken.

**3. Top with the cream cheese.** Place the block of cream cheese right on top (no need to cut it up—it'll melt when it's ready).

**4. Cook.** LOW: 4 to 6 hours. HIGH: 2 to 3 hours. Cook until the chicken is very tender and easy to shred.

**5. Shred and stir.** Using two forks, shred the chicken in the slow cooker, and then stir everything together until chicken mixture turns into a creamy, dreamy situation.

**6. Serve.** Spoon it over rice, pile it on buns, stuff it in a baked potato, or eat it straight from the bowl while standing at the counter. (No judgment. That's how most good recipes are tested.)

## Kitchen Tips

* Don't overthink the ranch seasoning. "Heaping" is the correct measurement here. If you love ranch, add a little more. Measure with your heart.
* If the sauce feels too thick, stir in a splash of chicken broth or 1 to 2 tablespoons of milk to loosen it up.
* Make Ahead: Cook as directed, shred, stir, and store in the fridge. It reheats beautifully.
* Store: Refrigerate leftovers in an airtight container up to 4 days.
* Freeze up to 2 months. Thaw overnight in the fridge.
* Reheat: Warm on the stovetop over low heat or microwave in short bursts, stirring in between. Add a splash of milk if needed to bring it back to creamy.

# The Knife in Hand

*(If blood makes you squeamish, y'all, you might want to skip this one!)*

Six days before Christmas—when life is already loud, the calendar is already crowded, and every mother is operating on caffeine and a prayer—I decided I was going to be *that* mom. You know the one: The warm, magical, "yes I made the hot chocolate bar" mom. The mom who shows up to the classroom party with marshmallows and sprinkles like she just stepped out of a Hallmark movie.

I had exactly 46 minutes to make it happen and get it to my son's school. Which is not "plenty of time." That is "panic." I had all the ingredients laid out: cocoa, condensed milk, evaporated milk, heavy cream, the fun toppings, and the whole cozy dream. The only thing I did *not* have . . . was a can opener.

Now listen—before you judge me, I open evaporated milk cans the old-school way. By stabbing them with a knife. Because that's how I've seen my grandmother do it a thousand times, and if you grow up watching a woman do something confidently, you start to believe it is not only safe, but also *the law.*

Plus, evaporated milk cans—can we talk about them? Why are they still living in 1904? Who is responsible for their design? We have phones that recognize our faces, cars that park themselves, and robots vacuuming our floors . . . but evaporated milk cans still don't have a tab. A TAB.

We are trying to pour liquid out of them. The goal should not be to fight for our lives. There should be a flip-top on the can—like a soda—so you can pour out the amount you need without injury, drama, or stitches. But apparently nobody has informed the evaporated milk people that modern technology exists.

So, there I am, in a hurry, standing in my kitchen with the confidence of a woman who has never met consequences. I grab a steak knife. I stab the can. First puncture—perfect. Success. I'm feeling proud. Like, Look at me, carrying on tradition. I am domestic. I am capable. I am highly favored. But you have to make two holes. One hole is for pouring, and the second hole is for the air to escape, or else the milk won't flow. I'm sure you already knew that, because you seem smart and safe and probably own a can opener. So, I go to stab the second hole. The knife hits the top of the can and makes a tiny dent. It does not puncture. And in my rushed little Christmas-party brain, I think: *Okay. Stab harder.*

And this is where everything goes wrong—because rushing always makes you think the solution is "more force," when the solution is actually "slow down and look." I look away for half a second—because I enjoy living dangerously I guess—and I go for the second stab. And my aim has not always been great.

So instead of puncturing the can . . . I puncture something much softer than a can should be. I look down and see our steak knife sticking out of my hand—wedged right in that webby spot between my forefinger and my thumb. And my soul leaves my body. It doesn't float. It doesn't drift. It exits.

I stare at my hand, stare at the knife, and think, *Oh. This is how I perish. In my own kitchen. Over evaporated milk.* I pull the knife out—because panic makes you do things without consulting a medical professional—and blood goes everywhere.

And I mean . . . everywhere. And the worst part? I don't even have a shirt on. Because I had taken my shirt off to throw it in the dryer to get wrinkles out, since irons do not exist in my household. We don't iron. We tumble and hope. We fluff and trust. Plus, it's warm when you get it out of the dryer and put it on, and that feels like a hug. So, I'm standing in my kitchen in pants and a sports bra, no shirt, bleeding like a stuck hog, clutching my hand and whispering, "No no no no no."

I do the only thing I know to do: Elevate my hand above my heart and apply pressure. I apply pressure. I breathe. I tell myself I'm fine. Then, I remove the pressure to check it—because I am nosy, even about my own injuries—and I look into the hole. And I see straight down to muscle. I almost pass out. Now I can handle anything. I can handle bodily fluids. I went through nursing school—part of it anyway—that's another story for another day.

I can deal with all kinds of gross things . . . Except when they're coming out of my own body. That is where I draw the line. So, I call my husband, Seth, in a full state of shock and holiday chaos. "I don't know what to do," I tell him through labored breathing. "I stabbed myself. I'm not sure where I should go. I don't have a shirt on. I'm losing consciousness. I'm bleeding bad. Tell the children I love them." I was extremely dramatic.

Seth—steady as always—asks, "Can you drive?"

And I'm like, "Maybe. Once I get a shirt on. HOW AM I GOING TO GET A SHIRT ON WHEN I AM BLEEDING AND ALSO COMPLETELY DELUSIONAL?"

And he says, "Okay. Get a shirt on. Wrap your hand tight. Get in the car. I'll meet you at urgent care. Everything's going to be fine."

Now here's what my brain hears in that moment: *But the hot chocolate bar.* Because when you're a mom, you can be actively bleeding out and still think, *I have obligations.* I'm sitting there like, *Lord, I might lose my hand, but I cannot let these children down.*

So, I drive to urgent care with my hand wrapped up, trying not to faint, trying not to cry, trying not to look at the wound because I am one glance away from meeting Jesus in the driver's seat. And on the way there, my entire hand does this weird muscle spasm thing—like the muscle is angry because it has been antagonized by a knife. It twitches and cramps and seizes, and I think, *Well. There it goes. My hand is about to fall off. Just right here on the road like a salamander tail.* Luckily, it did not.

I pull into urgent care, and when they see me walking in with blood dripping, they decide it is, in fact, pretty urgent. They check me in immediately.

Wonderful staff. Wonderful care team. They take me back, unwrap my hand, and one look at the gaping hole tells them everything. "Yes, ma'am," the doctors say. "You are definitely going to need stitches and probably a tetanus shot, just in case." And then—because my life is a sitcom—my dear friend who works there walks in, sees me, and we recognize each other immediately. And bright as day, she says, "Hey Meghan! I actually need to practice my stitch skills . . . would you mind if I practiced on your hand?"

Practice. On my hand. Like my hand is a worksheet. Like I am a Thanksgiving turkey. Like we're doing arts and crafts. I blink at her and say, "How quick can you sew? Because I'm supposed to have a hot chocolate bar at my kid's school in half an hour."

And she promises, "Oh we can get you there." And I'm thinking, *Ma'am. You are talking like this is a field trip.* But listen—by the time the lidocaine shot hit my hand, I was giggly.

Because that's what I do when I'm overwhelmed. I start laughing. I start cracking jokes. I start acting like I'm fine even when there is a hole in my body. I asked my friend if she could sew an "M" into my hand like a monogram.

She said she could not. So, she stitched me up, and I made it through, and my hand stayed attached to my body—praise God. And here's the lesson I walked out with: Do not rush through life. Because when you rush, you make mistakes. When you rush, you stop paying attention.

When you rush, you start moving with confidence instead of clarity. And confidence is cute until you stab yourself nearly through the hand with a steak knife over evaporated milk.

The kitchen is not the place for autopilot. It's not the place for "I'll just do it fast." It's not the place for "I've done this before." That's how you turn a wholesome Christmas hot chocolate bar into an urgent care trip.

So yes—I did, in fact, still get the hot chocolate bar to my son's school. I did not use the original hot chocolate base, obviously, because I wasn't about to roll up with a pot of "may contain traces of blood."

I tossed the whole batch. I used a totally different pot. I started over. And funny enough . . . it might have been the best hot chocolate I have ever made.

Because the second time around, I was slow. I was intentional. I was paying attention. I was fully aware that life is precious and steak knives do not forgive. And I learned my lesson: Don't rush—and don't use a knife on a can that should've been redesigned 20 years ago.

The End.

# Cheesy Bacon & Corn Casserole

SERVES 10 TO 12

**prep:** 15 minutes | **cook:** 25 minutes | **total:** 40 minutes

*This is one of those casseroles that tastes like a hug. It's creamy, salty, cheesy, and full of bacon and corn. And listen, you can skip the Ritz topping. You can. But then you'll have to live with that decision.*

- 1 (12-ounce) package center-cut bacon, chopped
- ½ cup (1 stick) salted butter
- ⅓ cup all-purpose flour
- 1½ cups whole milk
- 1 (8-ounce) block cream cheese, softened and cubed
- 1 to 1½ cups shredded Cheddar cheese (freshly shredded if you love yourself)
- 3 (15.25-ounce) cans whole-kernel corn, drained well

CRACKER TOPPING (optional, but encouraged)

- 1 sleeve buttery round crackers,* crushed
- 3 tablespoons salted butter, melted

**1. Preheat and prep.** Preheat your oven to 350°. Lightly spray a 13x9-inch baking dish with cooking spray.

**2. Cook bacon.** In a large, heavy skillet, cook chopped bacon until crisp over medium heat. Transfer bacon to a plate. Carefully drain off most of the bacon drippings, leaving about 1 to 2 tablespoons in the pan for flavor.

**3. Make the roux.** Add the butter to the skillet. Once melted, whisk in the flour until smooth. Cook for 1 minute, whisking, so it doesn't taste like raw flour.

**4. Make the sauce.** Slowly pour in the milk while whisking constantly. Keep whisking until the mixture thickens into a smooth, creamy sauce, 2 to 4 minutes.

**5. Add the good stuff.** Stir in the cream cheese until fully incorporated. Add the shredded Cheddar, and stir until smooth. Stir in corn and bacon until everything is coated. Pour into the prepared dish, and spread evenly.

**6. Optional cracker topping.** Mix crushed crackers with melted butter, and sprinkle over the top.

**7. Bake it hot.** Bake until hot and bubbly, 25 minutes.

**I used Ritz crackers.*

## Kitchen Tips

- Drain the corn well or you'll water down the sauce, and we can't have that.
- If your cream cheese is cold, it'll melt slower—cube it up, and let it sit out for 10 minutes if you can.
- Want a little kick? Add a pinch of cayenne or a few dashes of hot sauce to the sauce.
- If using the cracker topping, crush the crackers unevenly for the best texture.
- Make Ahead: Assemble (without crushed cracker topping), cover, and refrigerate up to 24 hours. Add crushed cracker topping right before baking.
- Storage: Refrigerate leftovers covered for 3 to 4 days.
- Reheat: Warm in a 350° oven until heated through, or microwave individual servings. Add a few fresh crushed crackers on top if you want to bring back the crunch.

# Broccoli & Cheese Casserole

SERVES 10 TO 12

**prep:** 15 minutes | **cook:** 15 minutes | **total:** 30 minutes *(plus rice cook time if needed)*

*This recipe takes me straight back to childhood—it's warm, buttery, and covered in crackers. This is comfort food with a capital C. And yes, we are using Cheez Whiz—that glorious plastic cheese—because it tastes fantastic in this recipe. I will not be accepting complaints today. Thank you.*

**Softened butter, for the baking dish**
**1 onion, chopped**
**1 cup rice (see note below)**
**1 (8-ounce) can processed cheese spread***
**1 (10.5-ounce) can cream of mushroom soup**
**½ cup (1 stick) salted butter, melted**
**2 (12-ounce) bags frozen broccoli florets**
**Buttery round crackers***

**1. Preheat and grease.** Preheat your oven to 350°. Butter a 13x9 inch baking dish.

**2. Prep the base.** In a medium skillet, sauté chopped onion over medium heat until translucent, about 4 to 6 minutes. In a large bowl, combine rice, sautéed onion, cheese spread, cream of mushroom soup, and melted butter. Stir until smooth and fully combined. Fold in broccoli florets until coated. Pour mixture into the prepared dish, and spread evenly.

**3. Top with crackers.** Crush crackers (in the bag—because we're efficient), and sprinkle generously over the top. There is no strict limit on crackers. Let your spirit guide you.

**4. Bake and serve.** Bake until hot and bubbly and the top is lightly golden, 15 minutes. Serve warm.

**I use Cheez Whiz (yes ma'am, yes sir) and Ritz crackers.*

**Rice Note:** If using instant rice, no need to cook first. If using regular long-grain rice, cook according to package directions, and let cool slightly.

## Kitchen Tips

* This recipe is flexible: You can add shredded chicken, diced ham, or even extra onions if you're feeling brave.
* Make Ahead: Assemble everything except the crushed cracker topping. Cover and refrigerate up to 24 hours. Add crackers right before baking.
* Storage: Refrigerate leftovers covered for 3 to 4 days.
* Reheat: Warm in a 350° oven until heated through, or microwave individual servings. Add fresh crushed crackers on top if you want to revive the crunch.

Vegetable?
Dessert?
Identity crisis?
I support it."
*—Luci*

# Butter Pecan Sweet Potato Casserole

SERVES 10 TO 12

**prep:** 20 minutes *(plus baking sweet potatoes if making fresh)* | **cook:** 30 minutes *(plus 1 hour if baking sweet potatoes)*
**total:** 1 hour *(or about 2 hours if baking potatoes; includes 10 minutes resting)*

*I'm not handing you some run-of-the-mill sweet potato casserole that tastes like it came from a church potluck in 1983. Nuh uh. This is Butter Pecan Sweet Potato Casserole, honey. And you already know my philosophy: more butter, more better. If you're looking for restraint, this is not your casserole. This is a holiday hug with a pecan crown.*

---

**Softened butter, for the baking dish**

**FILLING**

- **3 cups mashed sweet potatoes (see note below)**
- **½ cup granulated sugar**
- **½ teaspoon salt**
- **2 large eggs, well beaten**
- **1 teaspoon vanilla extract**
- **½ teaspoon ground cinnamon**
- **½ cup salted butter, melted**

**BUTTER PECAN TOPPING**

- **½ cup salted butter, softened**
- **⅔ cup packed dark brown sugar**
- **½ cup all-purpose flour**
- **1 cup pecans, chopped**

---

**1. Preheat and grease.** Preheat your oven to 350°. Butter an 11x7-inch baking dish. Make sure it's deep.

**2. Make the filling.** In a large bowl, whisk together mashed sweet potatoes, sugar, salt, beaten eggs, vanilla, cinnamon, and melted butter. Whisk until smooth and fully combined.

**3. Assemble.** Spread the sweet potato filling evenly into the prepared dish.

**4. Make the topping.** In a separate bowl, combine butter, brown sugar, flour, and chopped pecans. Use a fork (or your fingers) to mix until crumbly—like a streusel.

**5. Top it.** Sprinkle the topping evenly over the sweet potato filling, covering the whole surface. No bald spots. We want full pecan coverage.

**6. Bake and serve.** Bake until the topping is set and golden and the edges are bubbly, 30 minutes. Let rest 10 minutes before serving (it thickens as it cools).

**Sweet Potato Note:** You can use canned mashed sweet potatoes, or you can boil peeled sweet potatoes. But for the best flavor, bake the sweet potatoes. Bake at 400° for about 1 hour, until very tender. Cool, peel, mash.

## Kitchen Tips

* Add a pinch of salt to the topping to balance the sweetness and make everything pop.
* Chop pecans to your preference: finer for a more uniform crunch, bigger pieces for that "butter pecan ice cream" vibe.
* If the top starts browning too fast, loosely tent with foil for the last 10 minutes.
* Make Ahead: Bake and mash sweet potatoes up to 2 days ahead. Refrigerate.
* Assemble the casserole (without baking), cover, and refrigerate up to 24 hours. Bake as directed, adding 5 to 10 minutes if it's cold from the fridge.
* Storage: Refrigerate leftovers covered for 3 to 4 days.
* Reheat: Warm in a 350° oven until heated through, or microwave individual servings. (The oven keeps that topping crispier.)

# Pineapple Casserole

SERVES 8 TO 10

**prep:** 15 minutes | **cook:** 30 minutes | **total:** 50 to 55 minutes *(includes resting)*

*Let me ask you something: Have you ever met two ingredients and thought, Absolutely not. Y'all don't go together. And then you watched them show up, match energies, enhance each other's best qualities, and suddenly, you're like . . . Wow. I've been judgy as crap." That is pineapple casserole. The main characters are pineapple and Cheddar cheese—yes, I heard you gasp—but together, they become sweet-and-salty perfection. Consider this your reminder that sometimes the best things in life are the ones you didn't understand at first glance.*

---

**Softened butter, for baking dish**
**2 (20-ounce) cans pineapple chunks in juice (see tips below)**
**1 cup granulated sugar**
**5 tablespoons all-purpose flour**
**1 cup freshly shredded sharp Cheddar cheese**
**½ cup (1 stick) salted butter, melted**
**1 sleeve buttery round crackers,* crushed**
**Garnish: chopped fresh parsley**

---

**1. Preheat and grease.** Preheat your oven to 350°. Butter an 8x8-inch baking dish.

**2. Prep the pineapple.** Drain pineapple, and reserve 6 tablespoons pineapple juice.

**3. Make the sweet base.** In a mixing bowl, whisk together sugar, flour, and the reserved pineapple juice until smooth. Stir in the drained pineapple chunks until coated. Pour pineapple mixture into the prepared dish.

**4. Add cheese.** Sprinkle shredded Cheddar evenly over the pineapple layer.

**5. Make the topping.** In a medium bowl, combine melted butter and crushed crackers. Sprinkle buttery crushed cracker mixture evenly over the cheese.

**6. Bake and serve.** Bake until golden on top and bubbly around the edges, 30 minutes. Let rest 5 to 10 minutes (it sets up and behaves better after a short rest). Garnish with parsley before serving.

**I use Ritz crackers.*

## Kitchen Tips

* Canned pineapple works best here—it's softer and sweeter, and this casserole likes that.
* Want it more dessert-like? Serve warm with vanilla ice cream, and watch people question their entire belief system.
* Want it more savory? Use extra-sharp Cheddar, and add a pinch of salt to the pineapple mixture.
* This pairs beautifully with ham, turkey, or anything smoked. Pineapple casserole loves a holiday.
* Make Ahead: Assemble the pineapple and cheese base (without the cracker topping), cover, and refrigerate up to 24 hours. Add the cracker topping right before baking for maximum crunch.
* Storage: Refrigerate leftovers covered for 3 to 4 days.
* Reheat: Warm in a 350° oven until heated through. If you want the topping crisp again, add a small handful of fresh crushed crackers for the last 5 minutes.

"This is either genius or a cry for help. Either way . . . I'm getting seconds."

*—Luci*

# Lindsey and the Giant Peach

My friend Lindsey is one of those people you meet and immediately think, *Oh. She's a safe place.* She is genuinely beautiful—inside and out. Her heart is pure. Her spirit is kind. She looks for the best in people the way some folks look for their keys: relentlessly, faithfully, and with the full belief that goodness is always nearby. She is wonderful.

Except . . . she has the palate of a 6-year-old. And I don't say that to shame her—I say that as a statement of fact, like "the sky is blue" and "Florida has 12 seasons" and "Lindsey will choose chicken nuggets even if the menu is 12 pages long and features handmade truffle pasta."

Now, in our long-standing friendship, Lindsey has grown. She has branched out. She has evolved. Not drastically. But noticeably. Lindsey has gone from ordering chicken nuggets and fries . . . to still ordering chicken nuggets and fries but also sampling whatever weird food is on my plate. Which is huge.

Because I have an adventurous palate, I will try *anything* once. I'm the type of person who sees "Squid Ink Mafaldine" and thinks, *Yes. Put it directly in my mouth. I want to taste the ocean's wildest fare.* Lindsey, however, has historically felt safest when her food looks like it came from a kid's menu.

So, when she started leaning over and side-eyeing my plate like, *What is that? Do you like it? Can I smell it?*—I knew we were making progress. That's why, when we had a girls' night in Tallahassee, and I was responsible for booking dinner reservations, I had a plan.

I booked us at Il Lusso—an upscale restaurant with an Italian flair that promises the kind of steaks and pastas that make you sit up straight and whisper, "Okay . . . this is fancy." It was perfect. Lindsey could order a good steak. Safe. Elegant. Familiar.

And I could order my favorite: Squid Ink Mafaldine. Girls' night meant we were going all out. It meant we were going to laugh too loud, stay too late, and order appetizers like we had a trust fund.

Our waiter, Alexander, came over and started reciting the specials like he was narrating a romance novel. And then, he said something that stopped me mid-sip: "A peach dish . . . with sushi-grade fish . . . and accompaniments.:"

Now when someone says "peach" and "fish" in the same sentence, you have two options:

1. You run

2. You lean in

I leaned in. It sounded like one of the oddest dishes I'd ever heard in my life. The kind of dish that's either going to be a spiritual experience . . . or a story you tell for years.

So, I ordered arancini—because if arancini is on the menu, I am ordering it. That is my rule.

But we also told Alexander, "Yes. Please put in an order for the peach and fish . . . *conglomeration*."

We sipped and giggled and chatted, perusing the entrée portion of the menu like we were making decisions for the United Nations. Lindsey was feeling herself. I was feeling myself. We were thriving. And then, the appetizers arrived. Y'all. The plating was gorgeous.

It was one of those dishes where you immediately understand why people say, "You eat with your eyes first," because my eyes were full.

Thin, delicate slices of what appeared to be peaches were laid out in a perfect circle. Matching slices of fish layered right alongside them. Avocado crema. Microgreens. Edible flowers. It looked like the kind of dish you post on Instagram with a caption like: *Savoring the little things.*

Meanwhile, you're just trying not to drop your fork. I could feel Lindsey's eyes locked onto it. She was staring like she wanted to understand it. Respect it. Maybe even befriend it. "I do love a peach," she said.

"Mmhmm," I nodded. "They are good. Take a bite." Now, before I tell you what happened next, I need to clarify something: In the low mood lighting, I could not tell which slice was peach and which slice was fish.

And you would think that would be obvious. You would think, *Meghan, surely you can identify a fruit.* But no. The lights were dim. The dish was artistic. The slices were similar in shape and thickness. The mood lighting was low and the stakes were high.

Lindsey lifted her fork like a woman stepping into bravery. She gently speared what she believed was a peach—because it was soft-looking and beautiful and innocent—and she put the entire thing straight into her mouth. And I watched it happen in slow motion.

Like a nature documentary. But also like a tragedy. Do you know what it's like to expect sweet tea and take a sip of Coca-Cola? That shock? Multiply it by 40. Because Lindsey was expecting peach. And what she got . . . was raw fish.

And here's the thing about Lindsey: She was raised with couth. With scruples. With manners. She is not the kind of woman who spits something out in public. Lindsey will choke politely before she embarrasses herself.

So, the chicken-nugget-and-french-fry girl had just consumed sushi-grade fish for the first time in her natural born life . . . and she froze. I watched her face go from peaceful to horrified in 0.08 seconds.

She stared straight ahead like her soul had left her body and gone to sit in the car. She chewed. She drank. She swallowed.

And I sat there in stunned silence watching my friend complete the most courageous act of her life. I leaned in and whispered, "Are you okay?"

She swallowed again, eyes wide, and gagged quietly—like a lady. "I don't think . . . " she rasped, ". . . that was a peach."

"What?" She turned to me, whisper-yelling through pure betrayal.

"I DO NOT THINK THAT WAS A PEACH, MEGHAN."

And she was correct. 'Twas not a peach. But she tried it. And honestly? The dish was good. Light. Fresh. Bright. It tasted like summer with a college degree. It just wasn't chicken. And for Lindsey, that is a major detail.

But here's the wisdom in this ridiculous little moment: Sometimes growth doesn't look like a giant leap. Sometimes it looks like a friend taking one brave bite . . . and surviving it with dignity. Sometimes it looks like trying the weird thing, even if you don't end up loving it. Sometimes it looks like being willing to step outside your comfort zone —just enough—to discover you're tougher than you thought.

And also: It's okay to not like everything. Trying something new doesn't mean you have to become a new person overnight.

It just means you were brave for a minute. And Lindsey? She was brave. She didn't become a sushi girl. She didn't suddenly start ordering "crudo" and "tartare" and saying things like, "I love the mouthfeel." But she did try it. And that's the point.

Because life is like a menu—if you only ever order what feels safe, you might miss something wonderful. Or at least, you'll miss a hilarious story that will keep your friends entertained for the next decade. So, in honor of Lindsey's Great Peach Fish Incident of Tallahassee . . .

I'm offering a safer tribute. A more *Lindsey-friendly* tribute. Because while Il Lusso gave us peaches and sushi-grade surprises, I'm here to give you peaches the way the good Lord intended: warm, sweet, and nowhere near anything that swims.

So instead of recreating that fancy little peach-and-fish situation . . . we're pivoting. We're redeeming the peach. We're bringing her back home to her Southern roots. Here is my Peach Cobbler recipe—soft, buttery, bubbling around the edges, and guaranteed to taste like comfort instead of confusion.

And who knows? Maybe Lindsey will try it. Maybe she'll even love it. And if not? Well . . . at least we can all agree it's definitely a peach this time.

# Peach Cobbler

SERVES 8 TO 10

**prep:** 10 minutes | **cook:** 40 to 50 minutes
**total:** 1 hour 5 minutes to 1 hour 15 minutes *(includes cooling)*

*This is the cobbler I put together when I need something warm, sweet, and guaranteed to make people act like they've never eaten dessert before. Also: The don't stir part feels wrong the first time. Trust me. Southern science is at work.*

**½ cup (1 stick) salted butter**
**1 cup self-rising flour**
**1 cup granulated sugar**
**1 cup whole milk**
**1 (29-ounce) can sliced peaches in heavy syrup, undrained**
**1 teaspoon ground cinnamon (optional, but cozy)**
**Ice cream, to serve**

**1. Preheat and grease.** Preheat your oven to 350°. Place the stick of butter in a 13x9-inch baking dish, and slide it into the oven until fully melted.

**2. Mix your batter.** In a medium bowl, whisk together self-rising flour, sugar, and milk until smooth.

**3. Add batter.** Carefully remove the hot dish from the oven. Pour the batter directly over the melted butter. Do not stir. Not even a little swirl.

**4. Add peaches.** Spoon the undrained peaches and syrup evenly over the top. Again: Do not stir. The batter will rise up like it has something to prove.

**5. Optional cinnamon moment.** Sprinkle cinnamon over the top if you want that warm, bakery-smell energy.

**6. Bake it.** Bake until the top is golden and the edges are bubbly and syrupy, 40 to 50 minutes.

**7. Cool a bit.** Let cool 15 minutes so the sauce can thicken up and behave. Serve warm with ice cream.

## Kitchen Tips

* The rule is simple: If you stir it, you're making something else. Still tasty. But not cobbler.
* Want it extra crispy on top? Bake closer to 50 minutes, and let it rest the full 15 minutes.
* No self-rising flour? Use 1 cup all-purpose flour + 1½ teaspoons baking powder + ¼ teaspoon salt.
* Make Ahead: Bake earlier in the day, and let it sit at room temp for a few hours. Warm it before serving.
* Storage: Cover and refrigerate up to 4 days.
* Reheat: Warm servings in the microwave, or reheat the whole dish at 300° for 15 to 20 minutes.
* Freeze: Technically yes (up to 2 months), but the topping softens. I prefer fresh or fridge-leftovers.
* Serve warm with vanilla ice cream—because peaches and cream is delightful.

# Living in the Blessing

Some people arrive in your life with sunshine and butterflies and a little Pinterest quote on their tongue. Kallie arrived with *life experience*, a protective layer of sarcasm, and a worldview that basically said, "Hope is cute, but I don't trust it." And truthfully? I didn't blame her.

Kallie has been through more than most people endure in a lifetime. I'm not going to share her story in detail because that is hers to tell, but when I say she's had it hard, I mean hard. The kind of hard that can make you stop expecting good things—not because you're bitter, but because expecting hurts when you keep getting disappointed. So yes, she leaned cynical. Cynical is just what happens when your heart has had to put on steel-toe boots. Kallie came to work with us in the office—beautiful, smart, hilarious, capable—and she was a very proud agnostic. She had essentially concluded: *The world is not good, and if God is real, He's not paying attention.* Then . . . there was me.

Hi, I'm Meghan. I'm the girl with the big laugh and the bigger optimism. I'm the one who will cry in the car, pray through it, put on lip gloss, and still show up smiling because I truly believe better days are coming. And let me clarify: Joy does not mean life is easy. Joy means I have learned how to hold on to hope with both hands. It's the way I live. I call it "living in the blessing."

Now, I can hear some of y'all already: *"Meghan . . . be so for real."* I am for real. Because "living in the blessing" isn't me pretending everything is perfect. It's me believing God is still good, even when life isn't. It's me choosing to notice the small mercies. The tiny wins. The little surprises that whisper, *Hey . . . you're not forgotten.* And all you have to do is accept it. That's the part people overcomplicate—because we're human, and we love making everything harder than it needs to be. We will stare at a blessing like it's suspicious. We'll interrogate it. We'll call it luck. We'll say, "Well, we didn't earn it." But a blessing is still a blessing, even if you don't understand it.

Kallie and I clicked almost immediately. Not because we agreed on everything—we didn't—but because she had a good heart and an open mind, and I'm not the kind of person who bases friendship on whether or not you check the same boxes as me. I just loved her.

And she loved me too . . . even though she made fun of me. Because early on, she started noticing a phrase I say without even thinking. People would ask, "Hey Meghan, how are you?"

And I'd respond, "Oh, you know . . . just living in the blessing." And Kallie would scoff like I had just said something totally absurd. She didn't just laugh. She *scoffed*.

Like, "Ma'am. Stop it. You're embarrassing me." One day, we went to lunch at a little sandwich shop. We were talking about life, our views, our backgrounds—just getting to know each other deeper. I shared that I'm a Jesus follower, and that's where my joy comes from. She shared that she was . . . agnostic . . . maybe atheist . . . she wasn't sure.

And that's okay. I wasn't trying to slap a label on her; I was just trying to be her friend. I didn't care what she was. I just knew she needed to be loved. So, she talked about the things she'd been through, and I listened. I didn't minimize it. I didn't try to fix it with a Bible verse and a smile. I just sat in it with her. Because love doesn't rush somebody out of their pain. Love just stays. And then—right in the middle of that lunch—the owner walked by our table, set down a dessert, and said something like, "Hey, I just wanted y'all to have this." Just because. No reason. No occasion. No "you ordered this." Just . . . kindness.

And I looked at Kallie like I had been handed a microphone. I said, "Well look at that. All you have to do is accept it. That's living in the blessing." And she rolled her eyes so hard I thought they might fall into her tea. But I saw it. The tiniest crack in her cynicism. Just a little.

Later that same day, we were in a coworker's office talking about a certain international superstar—y'all know who she is. Sold-out arenas. Global icon. Married to a famous football player. You know. Her.

Kallie casually mentioned that seeing her perform live would be a bucket-list dream. She'd entered the ticket lottery before and never gotten them. "I'll never get tickets," she said, like she was stating a proven fact. And I don't know what came over me, but I said, "Just believe it. You'll get tickets." She looked at me like I was trying to sell her oceanfront property in Arizona.

"I will never get tickets," she repeated.

And I said, "Just believe. You're going to get tickets." Now I want to be clear: I wasn't trying to manifest anything with crystals and a vision board. I just . . . had this feeling. Like hope wanted to be spoken out loud. Well. I'll be dadgummed. That night someone called her and said, "I have an extra ticket. Do you want to go with me?"

Kallie walked into work the next morning looking like she'd seen a ghost. She told us the whole story, eyes wide, voice shaking. And I just smiled. And I said, "Look at you . . . living in the blessing." She rolled her eyes again, but this time, it had less bite. It had . . . wonder in it. And then, it started happening all the time.

Free appetizers. Random gifts. A front-row parking spot at the busiest places in town when the lot was full. (We call that princess parking.) One time, a new coffee truck opened up. Kallie showed me their posts, and said, "I wish I could try one of those coffees. They look so good. I would love one right now."

I said, "Yeah. Me, too. We'll get one." An hour later, the owner of that coffee shop walked into our office with coffees and donuts "for y'all to try." Kallie just stared at the cups like they were evidence in a courtroom. I said, "All you gotta do is accept it." She whispered, "This is weird."

I said, "No, this is Thursday." But my favorite day—the day I will never forget—was the lemon blueberry Bundt cake day. There was this lunch shop in town that kind of doubles as a bakery. They posted this lemon blueberry Bundt cake on their social media page. And when I tell you it was beautiful, I mean it looked like a dessert that had been blessed by a Southern grandmother and a French pastry chef at the same time. Kallie saw it.

Meanwhile, I happened to see the same post that day and thought, *You know what? The office would love that. They would go nuts over it.* So, I swung by right before closing. And I bought the last one.

The next morning, I carried that cake into the office like I was presenting the prize calf. I walked in and said, "You'll never guess what I got you."

Kallie said, "What?"

I said, "I stopped by that shop yesterday, and got you a lemon blueberry Bundt cake." Y'all. Kallie's jaw dropped so fast it nearly dislocated.

She said, "How did you know this?"

And I said, "Know what?"

She said, "I wanted one of these yesterday. I kept saying I wanted it. And they were sold out! They didn't have any!" And I just stood there holding the cake box like, *Well . . . would you look at God being sweet again.*

I said, "I don't know. I guess we live in the blessing." She stared at me for a long second. And then she smiled. Not a sarcastic smile. Not a "you're ridiculous" smile. A real smile. Like her heart had remembered how to hope.

That phrase—living in the blessing—started changing her. Not because I argued her into it. Not because I shamed her into it. But because I loved her through it. I listened. I stayed. I kept pointing at the little lights when she was used to living in the dark. And now?

Now, Kallie tells people she's living in the blessing. And she calls me laughing because some of her friends—people I've never even met—make fun of her for saying it. And we just smile. Because we know what it means. It means you start looking for the good again. It means you stop assuming everything will fall apart.

It means you let yourself believe you might be cared for—by people, by providence, by a God who hasn't forgotten your name. And here's the part that still makes me laugh, because of course it does—of course, this is how this story keeps unfolding. Years after "The Bundt Cake Incident" changed Kallie's entire outlook on life, I'm minding my business (which is rare for me), and I cross paths with the original baker who created that cake. The woman behind the magic. The patron saint of citrus and blueberries herself, Mrs. Vicki.

So, I did what any respectful Southern woman would do: I politely shot my shot. I asked her for the *actual* recipe card. Not a "measure with your heart, sweetie." The official, somebody's-been-making-this-since-forever recipe.

And wouldn't you know it—Mrs. Vicki handed it right over to me. Just . . . gave it to me. Which, if you ask me, is its own kind of blessing. Because getting the exact recipe from the original baker feels like being let into a family tradition you didn't even know you were allowed to have.

So, in honor of Kallie—my friend with a brave heart and a growing hope—and in honor of the day a Bundt cake read her mind and changed her heart—and in honor of Mrs. Vicki, who went ahead and made this whole thing official . . . Here it is. May it remind you that sweetness still exists. And maybe—just maybe—you're living in the blessing, too.

# Lemon Blueberry Bundt Cake

SERVES 10 TO 12

**prep:** 15 minutes | **cook:** 40 to 50 minutes | **total:** About 1 hour 15 minutes *(includes cooling)*

*This is the cake that feels like a little wink from Heaven. Bright lemon, juicy blueberries, and that kind of softness that makes people start confessing things at the kitchen counter. It's the perfect "just because" dessert—because sometimes the blessing shows up as tickets to a dream concert, and sometimes, it shows up as a Bundt cake that makes the whole office act right.*

Softened butter and flour (or baking spray) for the Bundt pan

CAKE

1 (13.24-ounce) box lemon cake mix

4 large eggs

Whole milk

1½ cups frozen blueberries

CREAM CHEESE ICING

2 (8-ounce) packages cream cheese, softened

1 cup (2 sticks) salted butter, softened

7 cups powdered sugar

Splash of vanilla extract (optional)

### MAKE THE CAKE

**1. Preheat and grease.** Preheat your oven to 350°. Butter and flour a 10-cup Bundt pan thoroughly. (Bundt pans love drama—don't give them the opportunity.)

**2. Mix the batter.** Mix the cake batter according to the box instructions but use 4 eggs and substitute milk for the water. Gently fold in the frozen blueberries. Don't overmix—you want blueberries, not purple batter.

**3. Bake.** Pour into the prepared Bundt pan, and bake until a toothpick inserted into the center comes out clean (a few moist crumbs are fine), 40 to 50 minutes. Let cake cool in the pan for 15 minutes, and turn out onto a wire rack to cool completely before icing.

### MAKE THE CREAM CHEESE ICING

**1. Whip the base.** In the bowl of a stand mixer fitted with a whisk attachment, beat the cream cheese and butter at medium speed until smooth and fluffy. Whip some air into it—this is how you get that light, cloudlike icing.

**2. Add the sugar.** With the mixer on low speed, add powdered sugar gradually until fully combined.

**3. Finish.** Increase mixer speed, and whip until fluffy. Add a splash of vanilla if you want, and ice the cooled cake.

## Kitchen Tips

* Frozen blueberries go in frozen. Thawing makes them juicy, and they'll turn your batter into a lavender situation.
* Grease your Bundt pan. Every ridge. Every crevice. No skipped spots.
* Whipping matters. The magic of this icing is air—whip it like you mean it.
* Make Ahead: Cake can be baked 1 day ahead. Ice the day of serving for the prettiest finish.
* Store: Refrigerate covered up to 5 days (cream cheese icing needs the fridge).
* Serve: Let slices sit at room temp 15 to 20 minutes for the best texture.

“Cut them small so you can eat six and still call it portion control.”

*—Luci*

# Chocolate Chip Squares

SERVES ABOUT 24 *(depending on how "generous" your squares are)*

**prep:** 10 minutes | **cook:** 20 to 25 minutes | **total:** 30 to 35 minutes *(plus cooling)*

*These are the bars that make people "just cut a sliver" and then immediately come back with a plate and no shame. This is my version of Congo Squares—I never really knew why they're called that. I just call them dangerous, because I could eat a whole pan in one sitting.*

**Softened butter, for baking sheet**
**2 cups packed light brown sugar**
**1 cup granulated sugar**
**1 cup unsalted butter, melted**
**2 large eggs**
**1 teaspoon vanilla extract**
**3 cups self-rising flour**
**12 ounces semisweet chocolate chips (about 2 cups)**

**1. Preheat and grease.** Preheat your oven to 350°. Butter an 11x15-inch baking sheet, and line with parchment paper for easy lifting.

**2. Make the batter.** In a large mixing bowl, whisk together the brown sugar, granulated sugar, melted butter, eggs, and vanilla until smooth and glossy. Add the self-rising flour gradually, mixing just until combined. (Don't overdo it—these bars like to stay soft and chewy.) Fold in the chocolate chips. Spread the batter evenly into your prepared pan.

**3. Bake until crusted.** Bake 20 to 25 minutes. Start checking at 20 minutes. They may not look done, but if you see a thin crust across the top and the center doesn't jiggle like soup, you're there. Cool completely before slicing (or cool mostly and slice anyway like the rest of us.)

## Kitchen Tips

* Don't overbake. If you wait until it "looks done," you'll end up with dry squares. Trust the top crust.
* Use parchment paper if you want clean slices and easy removal.
* Want to be fancy? Sprinkle a little flaky salt on top right when they come out of the oven.
* Make Ahead: Bake up to 2 days ahead—they get even chewier by day two.
* Store: In an airtight container at room tempature for 3 to 4 days.
* Freeze: Wrap tightly, and freeze up to 2 months. Thaw at room temp (or microwave a square for 10 to 15 seconds, and pretend it's fresh-baked).

# 5

# Family Legacy

This chapter is where we gather up what's left on the table and realize it was never just food. It was family. It was cousins running wild and making memories out of whatever the yard had to offer. It was breakfast traditions with Papaw, cinnamon-raisin biscuits, and the kind of small rituals that don't feel sacred until you're older and realize they were quietly building your heart the whole time. This chapter is about the love that made me, the people who shaped me, and the traditions I pray I never forget.

# Cousins, Character, and the Salad That Should Not Work

If you're an only child, you learn real quick how to be your own entertainment. You talk to yourself. You narrate your life like you're on a cooking show. You develop a rich inner world. And you also—if you're blessed—get cousins who basically become your built-in brothers and sisters.

Because when you're "the only one," your cousins are the closest thing you've got to siblings. And mine? Oh, they were it. Every weekend, like clockwork, Sabre, Skyler, and I would end up at Mamaw and Papaw's house. We'd ride bikes until our legs felt like noodles. We'd play outside until we were sticky, sunburnt, and feral. We were close in age, so it wasn't "cousins" energy—it was full-blown sibling energy. The kind where you love each other deeply . . . and also choose chaos recreationally. We did everything together. Beach camping. Mountain trips. Running wild like the yard was our personal kingdom and the grown-ups were just lucky to live in it. Those were the days where time moved slowly and summer felt endless and you could survive solely on hose water, saltine crackers, and tree swings.

Now, being close when you're young comes with a little mischief. And by "a little," I mean Sabre and I absolutely used our older-cousin authority irresponsibly. See, Skyler was the baby of the trio. I was the middle, and Sabre was the eldest, which meant Sabre and I were faster on bikes and . . . tragically overconfident. Sometimes we'd take Skyler out on bike trails and get going so fast that we'd leave him behind. And I need you to understand: We truly believed we were doing something noble. We told ourselves it was *character building*. We told ourselves, "He'll find his way home." We told ourselves, "This will teach him resilience." What we did not tell ourselves was: "This is how people end up on the evening news."

Looking back, I am horrified. Looking back, I'm like . . . *Why were we allowed outside unsupervised? Why did no one AirTag us? Why did we think the woods were a life coach?* But in the moment, we were proud. We were pioneers. We were wild little frontier women raising a tiny boy on survival skills he did not request. And it didn't stop at bike trails. No. Because we also had a passion for culinary arts. Enter: Rock & Grass Salad. Yes, that is exactly what it sounds like. We would gather "ingredients" from Mamaw and Papaw's yard—fresh-picked grass, a couple crunchy rocks for texture, maybe a leaf if we were feeling fancy—and we'd "serve" it to Skyler like we were running a five-star restaurant.

Now, whether he took a bite or not . . . I honestly can't remember. My memory is fuzzy, but my conscience is clear-ish. (Skyler, if you're reading this, I'm sorry. Also . . . you're welcome. You have grit now.) But that's what cousins do. They make your childhood louder. They make your weekends fuller. They give you someone to run with, laugh with, get in trouble with—and years later, they're still the people who know who you were before the world taught you to be polite. Cousins are special like that. They hold the whole history. And speaking of weird salads . . .

Let's talk about one that sounds like it came from the same creative team as Rock & Grass Salad—but I promise you, this one is actually edible and shockingly delicious. It's Mamaw's specialty. It's pears. And mayonnaise. And cheese. I know. *I know.* At first glance, it sounds like somebody got confused at the grocery store and just started grabbing things with confidence. It sounds like a dare. It sounds like something your great-aunt invented because she had five guests coming and exactly 12 minutes to impress them. But honey . . . it works. It's sweet and salty. Creamy and cold. It's got that little bite from the cheese and that soft, syrupy goodness from the pears. It's the kind of Southern "salad" that makes no sense until you've had one bite—and then you're standing there with your plate like, *"Well. I'll be. Hand me another."*

Because that's Southern food in a nutshell, isn't it? Sometimes it looks odd. Sometimes it might sound strange. Sometimes it has mayonnaise where mayonnaise should not be. But somehow, through the grace of God and the culinary bravery of our ancestors . . . it turns into something you crave. So, in honor of Sabre and Skyler—my not-siblings, my built-in best friends, my childhood co-conspirators—and in honor of every questionable "salad" that turned out to be a masterpiece . . . Let's make the pear one. The one that's weird on paper . . . but wonderful in real life.

“Pear Salad is proof that Southerners fear nothing.”

*—Luci*

# Pear Salad

**SERVES 5** *(2 pear halves per person)*

**prep:** 5 minutes | **total:** 5 minutes

*If you've never had pear salad, let me prepare you: This recipe looks like a prank and tastes like comfort. Sweet pears, a creamy little dollop of mayo, and sharp Cheddar on top—simple, strange, and somehow . . . perfect. Don't overthink it. Just try it.*

- **1 (29-ounce) can pear halves, drained well**
- **10 tablespoons mayonnaise (or one good dollop per pear half)**
- **1 to 1½ cups freshly shredded sharp Cheddar cheese**

1. **Pat the pears.** Pat the pear halves dry with a paper towel. (Yes, we're drying fruit. Trust the process.)
2. **Plate them pretty.** Place pear halves on a serving plate, cut side up.
3. **Add the dollop.** Spoon a dollop of mayonnaise right into the center of each pear half.
4. **Sprinkle the Cheddar.** Top each pear half with a generous sprinkle of Cheddar.
5. **Serve chilled.** Serve immediately.

## Kitchen Tips

- Shred your own cheese. This is not the time for bagged preshredded cheese with the "anti-caking" dust of sadness. Fresh Cheddar blends into the mayo like it was meant to be there.
- Pat the pears dry so your mayo doesn't slide off like it's trying to escape.
- Want to get fancy? Add a cracklin' of black pepper or a pinch of paprika on top.
- Make Ahead: You can assemble up to 2 to 4 hours ahead, and keep covered in the fridge.
- Storage: Best enjoyed the same day. If you must store leftovers, cover and refrigerate up to 24 hours—just know the pears can get a little weepy.

# Breakfast Traditions

Every Friday morning of my childhood, my life ran on one thing: Papaw's schedule. Not my mom's schedule. Not the school's schedule. Not the Lord's schedule. Papaw's. Because at 7 a.m. on the dot, that man would be waiting—engine running, coffee in hand, ready to escort me to the finest fast-food establishment in our small Southern town. Now, I know you're probably wondering what could be "fine" about eating a fast-food breakfast.

And before you judge us, just know this: It wasn't just breakfast. It was a tradition. It was a ritual. It was a weekly board meeting where a little girl and her Papaw handled important business—like biscuits, gravy, and what we would do if we ever won the lottery.

We did the same thing every week. We'd walk in, and he'd order me a biscuit and gravy like it was my birthright. Then—because we are nothing if not committed to joy—we'd order a cinnamon-raisin biscuit to share for what we called *breakfast dessert*. Because if you can't have dessert at 7:15 a.m. on a Friday, what are we even doing here?

When I was little, Papaw would cut up my biscuit and gravy for me. Small pieces, carefully, like he was preparing a meal for royalty. And I would sit there, swinging my feet under the booth, watching him like this was just what life was supposed to be: warm gravy, sweet bread, and somebody who loved you enough to make your food easier to eat. Then, I got older. And I started noticing things. Like . . . why is this man still cutting up my biscuit?

Because at 10 years old, you start thinking you're grown. You start believing the audacity you have. You start feeling mature because you can spell "responsibility" even though you don't have any. I remember being around that age and rolling my eyes internally like, *Papaw . . . I can cut my own biscuit and gravy. I am basically an adult.*

But I never said it. I just let him do it. Because deep down, even then, I knew it wasn't really about the biscuit. It was about him getting to take care of me in a way that didn't cost him anything but time. It was about love that showed up quiet and steady, with a plastic knife and a napkin.

And Papaw found joy in it. You could tell. He didn't do it because he thought I couldn't. He did it because he wanted to.

And then, like life does, the years started moving faster. School got busier. Priorities shifted. Mornings got crowded. And without any dramatic ending or big goodbye, our Fast-Food Fridays just . . . faded.

Not because we grew apart—we didn't. We just grew up, and sometimes, growing up means you accidentally set a tradition down and don't realize how long it's been sitting there.

Fast-forward about 14 years. I have my first baby. And from the moment my son entered this world, Papaw had one question—one goal—one mission: "So . . . when do you think he's old enough to go to breakfast with me?"

Not "How's the baby sleeping?" Not "How's your recovery?" Not "Do you need anything?" No. Breakfast.

Because in Papaw's mind, tradition isn't tradition until a new generation is eating gravy in a booth.

We waited until my son was potty trained, because if you've ever potty trained a toddler, you know you don't need to add public bathrooms into the mix. And fast-food restaurants, bless them, don't exactly offer diaper-changing stations with spa-like vibes.

So, when my son was about 3, Papaw started taking him out for breakfast. And y'all . . . he did the same thing for my boy that he did for me. Same routine. Same breakfast dessert. Same love.

Now my son is older, and he has spent nearly every Saturday solving the world's problems with the fast-food restaurant's crew. And I mean that literally. He has his people. His council. His breakfast board of directors.

He has watched them grow older. He has watched some of them transition into the next life. And as hard as that is, he's also learned something sacred:

You do not leave words unspoken.

You don't wait.

You don't assume you'll have another Saturday.

You tell people you love them while you can still sit across from them and pass the cinnamon-raisin biscuit back and forth. And, I like to think those sweet folks have gotten something from him, too—a reminder to see the world through a child's eyes. To laugh at small things. To get excited about breakfast dessert. To remember that joy doesn't have to be complicated.

It has been one of the most beautiful seasons to watch. And now my son is asking the same question I asked in my head all those years ago. "Mama . . . why is Papaw still cutting my biscuit up? I'm 10." And when he asked it, it hit me. Because I finally understand.

It's not that Papaw thinks my son can't do it. It's that Papaw doesn't *want* him to have to yet. Because when you're little, the world is lighter. When you're little, you don't carry bills and grief and responsibilities and the weight of everything you can't fix. When you're little, you can just be a kid who shows up on Saturday mornings and talks about life with people who love you.

And I think, in some small, quiet way, that's what Papaw is doing. He's keeping him young. He's holding onto that boyhood just a little longer, with a plastic knife and a gentle routine.

Because grown-ups have to cut their own biscuits. Kids get to be cared for. So, here's what I want to tell you—whether you're 10, or 30, or 70: Don't grow up too fast. You've got plenty of time.

The world will hand you heaviness soon enough—don't go looking for it early like it's a badge of honor. Let someone cut up your biscuit when they offer. Let the moment be sweet. Let the tradition be sacred. Just because you grow old doesn't mean you have to grow up.

And if you're blessed enough to have someone who still wants to take you to breakfast at 7 a.m. on the dot? Baby, take the ride. So, in honor of Papaw and childhood and breakfast dessert and the kind of love that shows up every week without fail . . .

Here is my recipe for Cinnamon & Raisin Biscuits. Make it on a slow morning. Share it with somebody you love. And if you're feeling sentimental . . . cut it up for them. They might roll their eyes.

But one day?

They'll understand.

# Cinnamon & Raisin Biscuits

## *(a.k.a. Fast-Food Breakfast Nostalgia, But Make It Homemade)*

**SERVES 9**

**prep:** 20 minutes | **cook:** 12 to 14 minutes | **total:** 42 to 44 minutes *(includes cooling)*

*These biscuits taste like Friday mornings, restaurant booth seats, and the kind of love that shows up at 7 a.m. on the dot. They're tall, fluffy, lightly sweet, warmly spiced, and studded with raisins that actually stay tender. And that glaze? It's not optional. It's the "breakfast dessert" part of the program. Here's how you honor tradition: Split one warm biscuit, add an extra drizzle of glaze (don't be shy), and eat it after your "real breakfast" like a responsible adult who still knows how to have joy.*

**BISCUITS**

- ¼ **cup salted butter, plus more for baking dish**
- ½ **cup raisins**
- 2 **cups self-rising flour**
- 2 **tablespoons granulated sugar**
- 1½ **teaspoons ground cinnamon**
- ¾ **to 1 cup cold whole buttermilk (or cold whole milk)**

**SIMPLE VANILLA GLAZE**

- ¾ **cup powdered sugar**
- 1 **to 2 tablespoons whole milk (as needed)**
- ½ **teaspoon vanilla extract**

**MAKE THE BISCUITS**

**1. Prep your ingredients.** Get everything for the biscuits cold. Place your butter, mixing bowl, and 2¼-inch biscuit cutter in the freezer while you prep. Put the raisins in a bowl, and cover with hot water. Soak 15 minutes, then drain, pat dry, and set aside.

**2. Preheat and grease.** Preheat your oven to 400°. Butter an 8x8-inch square baking dish.

**3. Make the dough.** In a medium bowl, whisk together self-rising flour, granulated sugar, and cinnamon. Grate the frozen butter into the chilled bowl, and gently stir until it's evenly distributed (you want little buttery bits everywhere—those are flavor pockets). Pour in ¾ cup cold buttermilk, and stir just until combined. Add more buttermilk, a splash at a time, if the dough is too dry. Stop as soon as the dough comes together. Fold in the raisins.

**4. Roll, fold, cut.** Turn dough onto a lightly floured surface, and roll to about ¾-inch thick. For tall biscuits: fold the dough in half, gently press/roll back out, and repeat 2 to 3 times. Cut biscuits with a floured and chilled round cutter, pressing straight down and lifting straight up (don't twist—twisting seals the edges and your biscuits will sulk instead of rise). Arrange biscuits snugly in the buttered dish.

**5. Bake.** Bake until the tops are lightly golden, 12 to 14 minutes.

**MAKE THE GLAZE**

**1. Glaze and serve.** Let biscuits cool in the pan 10 minutes. Whisk powdered sugar, milk (start with 1 tablespoon, add more as needed), and vanilla until smooth. Drizzle over warm biscuits, and enjoy immediately—preferably with someone you love.

## Kitchen Tips

* Cold dough = flaky biscuits. If your kitchen is hot, put the biscuits in the freezer for 5 minutes before baking.
* Soaking the raisins matters. It keeps them plump and soft instead of turning into tiny chewy interruptions.
* Snug in the pan is good. Biscuits baked close together rise taller and stay tender.

# Cinnamon Roll Casserole

SERVES 10 TO 12

**prep:** 15 minutes | **cook:** 35 to 40 minutes | **total:** 50 to 55 minutes *(plus 10 minutes resting)*

*It could be breakfast. It could be dessert. It could also be the reason your family suddenly starts attending brunch on time. All I know is: Somebody's going to ask you for the recipe before they finish chewing.*

CASSEROLE

- ½ cup (1 stick) salted butter
- 3 (12.4-ounce) cans refrigerated cinnamon rolls
- 4 large eggs
- ½ cup heavy cream
- 2 teaspoons ground cinnamon
- 2 teaspoons vanilla extract
- ¼ cup maple syrup

MAPLE GLAZE

- 3 tablespoons maple syrup
- ¼ cup bourbon (optional for the grown folks)

EASY CREAM CHEESE ICING (optional but highly recommended)

- 1 (8-ounce) block cream cheese, softened
- ½ cup (1 stick) salted butter, softened
- 4 cups powdered sugar
- Vanilla extract, to taste (start with 1 to 2 teaspoons)

MAKE THE CASSEROLE

1. **Preheat and grease.** Preheat your oven to 350°. Place the butter in a 13x9-inch casserole dish, and set it in the oven just until melted. Carefully remove.
2. **Prep the cinnamon rolls.** Open the cans, and set aside the icing packets. Cut each cinnamon roll into about 9 pieces. Scatter chopped cinnamon rolls evenly into the dish over the melted butter.
3. **Make the custard.** In a large bowl, whisk the eggs until combined. Add the heavy cream, cinnamon, and vanilla. Whisk together until smooth.
4. **Pour and drizzle.** Pour the custard evenly over the cinnamon rolls. Drizzle the maple syrup over the top.
5. **Bake.** Bake until puffed and golden brown on top and set in the center, 35 to 40 minutes.

MAKE THE MAPLE GLAZE

1. **Make the glaze.** In a small bowl, whisk together the reserved icing packets and 3 tablespoons maple syrup until smooth. Optional: Stir in bourbon if you want to take it from "Sunday school brunch" to "girls' weekend."

MAKE THE ICING (optional)

1. **Mix it smooth.** In a large bowl, beat the softened cream cheese and butter with a hand mixer on medium-low speed until smooth and fluffy. Add powdered sugar gradually (unless you enjoy wearing it). Mix until smooth. Add vanilla to taste, and mix again. Refrigerate until ready to serve.

ASSEMBLE

1. **Drizzle and serve.** Drizzle warm casserole with the maple glaze. Serve slices, and if you're doing life correctly, add a dollop of cream cheese icing on each serving right before eating.

## Kitchen Tips

- Don't use the large canned biscuits. This recipe needs the regular rolls so the custard bakes through evenly.
- For clean slices, let the casserole rest 10 minutes before cutting.
- Like it extra gooey? Pull it at 35 minutes. Like it more "set?" Go closer to 40 minutes.
- The bourbon is optional . . . but so is inner peace.
- Make Ahead: Assemble the casserole (up through pouring custard), cover, and refrigerate overnight. Bake the next morning; you may need to add 5 extra minutes since it's cold.
- Storage: Cover and refrigerate leftovers for 3 to 4 days. Store cream cheese icing separately in the fridge.
- Reheat: Microwave individual servings 20 to 30 seconds or warm in a 300° oven until heated through. Add glaze/icing after reheating for best texture.

# A Letter to My Parents

Before we get into this recipe, I need to talk to my parents for a minute. So, if you're reading this and you are not one of my parents . . . you can stay. But just know you're eavesdropping.

Respectfully. Mother and Daddy, I love y'all. And I know that sounds simple, but sometimes the simplest things are the truest, and also the hardest to say without my eyes tearing up.

Here's the thing: I didn't grow up in one of those neat little "Mom + Dad + kids + matching pajamas + everybody's emotional needs being met" situations. We didn't get the perfectly tied bow. We got . . . ribbon. In two different directions. With scissors involved.

Y'all split when I was in middle school, and I'm an only child—which means when the grown-ups start going through grown-up things, there isn't a sibling in the backseat to look at and silently mouth, *"Are you seeing this?"* It's just you.

Just you, in the middle, trying to be brave, trying to be good, trying to be easy to love . . . because somewhere in that young little brain you start thinking, *If I'm lovable enough, maybe this will hold.* That's not a kid's job. I know that now.

But back then? I was single-handedly trying to keep a family unit together like I was duct tape with bangs. And then, by my senior year of high school, it became official-official. The cord got cut. The paperwork got stamped. The "maybe" became a "no."

And I'm not going to lie—there's a part of that that still stings. Because I did have to grow up fast. I did carry things that were heavier than what a teenager should have to carry. I did learn how to read a room before I learned how to do my taxes. (And honestly, I'm still not great at taxes.)

But here is what I also know: Both of you were young. You married young. You did the best you knew how to do with the tools you had at the time. And the truth is, I don't hold a grudge. I don't.

Because life is hard, marriage is hard, and being human is . . . a full-time job with no lunch break. And even though we weren't a neat little nuclear family anymore, you both still chose me.

Out of everything you disagreed on—out of all the differences and the permanent uncoupling and the "we see the world completely opposite" moments—there was one thing you could always agree on: Me.

You both poured energy into making sure I felt loved. You both showed up. You both made sure I knew I mattered. And I am not blind to that. I'm not numb to it. I'm grateful for it. Because yes—those were some of the most traumatic seasons of my life.

But they also shaped me. They made me tender where I could have turned hard. They made me learn how to love people where they are. They made me become the kind of woman who tries to bring peace into a room instead of adding fuel to the fire.

And somehow, by the grace of God and the mercy of timing and the fact that y'all both genuinely love me . . . I got the best parts of both of you.

That's wild, honestly. Like genetically and emotionally, I should probably be a cautionary tale. But here I am. And, now let me talk about milk and cookies.

Because this recipe? This one takes me back. It takes me back to being a kid—back to the moments that were

good and soft and normal. Back to when the biggest problem in my life was whether the cookie was warm enough to melt the chocolate chips but not so warm that it would break in the milk.

This is one of those recipes that exists in the overlap. And it's a recipe I still remember—because some flavors stick with you, even when life changes shape. And that's what this dessert is, really: It's proof that just because something changes . . . it doesn't mean it was never real.

It's proof that love can look different and still be love. It's proof that you can be made from two people who couldn't stay together—and still grow up whole. This is milk and cookies layered into something new.

Not because the original wasn't good . . . but because sometimes life doesn't stay in one piece. Sometimes it becomes layers. And sometimes those layers—if you're gentle with them—turn into something beautiful.

So, Mother and Daddy . . . Thank you. For loving me. For choosing me. For raising me the best way you knew how. For making sure I never doubted I was yours.

And for the record—if y'all ever disagree again, just know this: I'm the only thing you ever made that came out perfect. Because even when everything was changing, even when I felt pulled in two directions, I never doubted that I was loved. And that mattered more than the shape our family took. It shaped me. It steadied me.

This recipe is my way of honoring that love—soft cookies dipped in milk and layered with a mascarpone cloud. Thank you for the best parts of you that you gave to me. Now come sit down.

I made dessert.

# Milk & Cookies Cake

SERVES 10 TO 12

**prep:** 25 minutes | **cook:** 10 to 12 minutes | **total:** 5 hourd *(includes cooling and chilling)*

*This is what happens when the classic milk-and-cookies dessert grows up and glows up. We're talking homemade chocolate chip cookies quickly dipped in milk and layered between a mascarpone and powdered sugar "cloud" that tastes like comfort and childhood—but with a little extra drama, the way the South intended.*

**CHOCOLATE CHIP COOKIES**

- 1 cup (2 sticks) unsalted butter, softened
- ¾ cup granulated sugar
- ¾ cup packed light brown sugar
- 2 large eggs
- 2 teaspoons vanilla extract
- 2¼ cups all-purpose flour
- 1 teaspoon baking soda
- 1 teaspoon salt
- 2 cups semisweet chocolate chips

**MASCARPONE CLOUD**

- 8 ounces cold mascarpone cheese
- 4 cups cold heavy cream, divided
- ¾ cup powdered sugar

**THE LAYERS**

- Whole milk, for dipping cookies (you'll use what you need)

MAKE THE COOKIES

**1. Preheat and grease.** Preheat your oven to 350°. Line large baking sheets with parchment paper.

**2. Mix the wet ingredients.** In a large bowl, cream the butter, granulated sugar, and brown sugar with a hand mixer on medium-low speed until fluffy, 2 to 3 minutes. Add the eggs one at a time, beating well after each addition. Stir in vanilla.

**3. Mix the dry ingredients.** In a separate bowl, whisk together the flour, baking soda, and salt.

**4. Make the dough.** Add the dry ingredients to the wet ingredients, and mix until just combined. Fold in the chocolate chips. Using a cookie scoop, scoop dough (about 2 tablespoons each) onto prepared baking sheets.

**5. Bake the cookies.** Bake until edges are set and centers still look a little soft, 10 to 12 minutes. Cool completely. (If you layer warm cookies, you'll have a delicious . . . mess.)

MAKE THE MASCARPONE CLOUD

**1. Prep your tools.** Chill your bowl (and whisk/beaters if you can). Cold tools = fluffy cloud.

**2. Whisk a cloud.** In the chilled bowl, add the mascarpone and 3 cups cold heavy cream. Whisk (or beat with a mixer at medium speed) until soft peaks form. Add powdered sugar. Continue whisking until you reach medium-stiff peaks—fluffy, smooth, and holding their shape.Refrigerate until ready to use (or up to 3 hours).

ASSEMBLE THE MILK AND COOKIES CAKE

**1. Prep your area.** Choose a cake stand (or something similar). Pour the milk into a shallow bowl.

**2. Dip the cookies.** Working with one cookie at a time, quickly dip each cookie in milk—for literaly 1 second. We are dipping, not baptizing.

**3. Layer the cake.** Arrange dipped cookies in a single layer on the bottom of the cake stand. Spread a generous layer of Mascarpone Cloud over the cookies. Repeat layers—cookies, cloud, cookies, cloud—until you use all the cookies.

**4. Cover and chill.** Cover and refrigerate at least 4 hours, preferably overnight, so everything softens into that perfect "sliceable but still spoonable" texture.

## Kitchen Tips

- Mascarpone is picky. Keep it cold, and don't overbeat or it can loosen up. Medium-stiff peaks means it holds shape, but it still looks soft and silky—not dry.
- If your cookies are super soft, you can skip dipping. Instead, drizzle milk lightly over the layers.
- Make Ahead: Best made the day before. It gets better as it rests.

# The First Miracle

Christmas Day 2025 was a historic occasion in our family for two reasons:

1. For the first time ever, I hosted *all* of my people at my house.
2. I nearly sent my very spiritual grandmother into the spirit realm . . . via bourbon ball.

Now, hosting Christmas is not for the faint of heart. It is a full production. It is a sugar-and-caffeine fueled marathon. It is you standing in your kitchen with flour on your shirt, a prayer on your lips, and 18 side dishes in your spirit. But it was brilliant. Truly. The whole family came to us. Everybody contributed a little something, and I—because I cannot help myself—made a full spread of Christmas goodies. Because why would we stop at lunch when we can also have enough tiny desserts that could feed a small nation? I'm talking: Sugar cookies. Chocolate cookie balls. Peanut brittle. Creamy fudge. Gingerbread truffles. And my personal favorite: Bourbon balls. Now, before we go any further, let me clarify something for the record—because my Mamaw would want it clarified, and because honesty is a spiritual gift whether you're spiritual or not.

I am NOT religious. At all. Matter of fact, I am very anti-religion. I am a Jesus follower. I don't live under the law of religion, I live in freedom. Let that marinate a minute. My Mamaw prefers not to be labeled as religious either—but she is very, VERY spiritual and a Jesus follower as well.

I walk in faith. I talk to God all the time. But I am not walking around with a tambourine and a binder of devotionals like I'm clocking in for duty. Mamaw lives in the "lay hands and rebuke in the grocery store if necessary" category.

I live in the "Lord, you know my heart" category. So yes—we are different flavors of faith in the same family pot. Which makes what happened next even funnier. Now let me be clear: My bourbon balls are not "bourbon flavored." They are bourbon *committed*. These are not the kind of treat you eat and go, "Mmm! A hint of bourbon!" No. These are the kind you eat and immediately feel your ancestors lean in like, *what are we doing?*

These bourbon balls will put hair on your chest whether you are male or female. They are little spheres of holiday cheer and reckless decision making.

The process alone should tell you they're serious. You pulverize pecans, and soak them for a full 24 hours in the strongest bourbon you can find—because in my recipe, we are not here to be delicate. Then you make a buttercream with those drunken pecans and add powdered sugar, butter, and—yes—more bourbon. Then you dip them in chocolate. I prefer dark chocolate because I like that little bitterness to balance the sweetness . . . and also because I enjoy living on the edge.

And to whoever needs to hear this: You do not cook the alcohol out. This is not a "bake it and it evaporates" situation. This is a "Jesus take the wheel" situation. Normally, when I take these to parties, I label them very clearly with a sign that says: "21+"

Now I am not out here carding folks like I'm working the door at the club, but I do my due diligence. I warn the people. I announce it with my mouth. I point. I gesture. I make eye contact. Because it's not about being legal . . . it's about being responsible.

Well, that year, my sweet grandparents were coming to my home for Christmas Day lunch. And y'all know they are precious. They are the kind of people who don't even like to sit too close to a rum cake.

My Mamaw, especially, has never consumed an

alcoholic beverage in her life. Or so she claims. And normally, when we do Christmas at their house, I don't bring my whole dessert circus because we already have enough food to qualify for disaster relief. But since everyone was coming to me this year—and we were in our new home—I thought: *We need lunch. We need dessert. We need a full Christmas spread.* Because why not?

Now, lunch was a success. We did our tradition: smoked steaks. It's our yearly thing, and it's glorious. Everybody ate. Everybody groaned. Everybody unbuttoned something. And afterward, people started grazing on the dessert table. That's when the problem began. Because I failed to label the truffles. And Mamaw wandered over, blissfully unaware, and plucked a bourbon ball thinking she had grabbed a chocolate cookie ball.

Now, in her defense, they look similar. They're both round. They're both covered in chocolate. They're both sitting there minding their business like little innocent angels. But one of them is basically a cookie. And the other one is a felony. She held it up and asked someone, "What is this?"

And—because the devil is a liar—someone replied, "Oh, it's just a truffle." *Just a truffle.* And I turned my head just in time to see my Mamaw pop half of that bourbon ball into her mouth. And I thought, *Oh no.* Because I know what's in those. I know the bourbon-to-ball ratio. I know the power those little chocolate grenades hold. So, I watched. I watched her bite down. And y'all . . . I saw it. I watched her face go from peaceful to . . . spiritually confused. Her eyes got big. She chewed slowly like she was trying to figure out whether she needed to rebuke it or swallow it. And I know she tasted it. I know her throat was burning. I know her soul was like, *Is this what the sinners are doing?*

She looked straight at me, cheeks full, and said: "Meghan . . . what's in this?"

And I said, as calmly as possible, "Oh. It's bourbon. A lot of bourbon. Matter of fact, that has alcohol in it." Now here's where my Mamaw impressed me: She did not spit it out. She did not gag. She chewed, grimaced, and swallowed like a woman who has been through too much in her life to be taken out by truffle. And I stood there wondering if I was about to witness the first Christmas in history where Mamaw got tipsy off one bite of dessert.

Like . . . was she about to start two-stepping to "Jingle Bell Rock"? Was she about to confess secrets? Was she about to look at Papaw and say, "Let's get wild"? I didn't know what was coming.

So, I asked, "Well . . . how did you like it?"

She said, "I didn't like it."

I said, "Not at all?"

She said, dead serious: "Meghan . . . that thing will give me a DUI from the passenger seat." And then she laughed. I laughed. Everyone within 10 feet laughed.

And I said, "Well, Mamaw, in my defense, I thought you could use a little bourbon to take the edge off. You always seem a little stressed around the holidays."

She looked at me sweet as pie and said, "Yes. Mainly because of you." And we laughed harder. And right there, in the middle of Christmas chaos, we had one of those moments that feels like a gift you get to keep. Just joy. Just family. Just a story that will get told every year from now until kingdom come.

So anyway—here's my recipe for the Bourbon Balls that almost sent my Mamaw into a new personality. Make them. Love them. But for the love of all things holy . . . label them. And be careful who you give them to.

# Bourbon Balls

**SERVES ABOUT 30** ***(depending on size and how many "samples" disappear)***

**prep:** 30 minutes *(plus chilling)* | **cook:** 5 minutes *(melting chocolate)* | **total:** 4 hours *(or overnight if you're living right)*

*These are the infamous bourbon balls—the ones I should've labeled, the ones Mamaw mistook for an innocent little "truffle," and the ones that can absolutely give you a DUI from the passenger seat if you're not paying attention. Fair warning: This recipe requires time, patience, and a willingness to forgive yourself when your hands get chocolatey and your attitude gets sanctified.*

---

- 2 cups pecans
- ¾ cup bourbon, divided
- 1 cup (2 sticks) salted butter, softened
- 1 (16-ounce) box powdered sugar (1 pound)
- 1 (16-ounce) bag dark chocolate melting wafers

---

**1. Soak the pecans.** Add the pecans to a food processor, and pulse until they're dust. (We're not making chunky nut confetti—this needs to be fine.) Transfer pecan dust to a bowl, and pour ½ cup bourbon over it. Stir well. Cover and refrigerate overnight if possible. If you're in a pinch, give it at least 2 hours.

**2. Make the bourbon ball "dough."** In a large mixing bowl, beat the butter with an electric mixer at medium-high speed until smooth. Add the powdered sugar gradually (unless you enjoy being baptized in sugar). Pour in the remaining ¼ cup bourbon (and yes, a tiny dash more is allowed). Mix until smooth and fully combined. Add the soaked pecans, and mix again until it becomes a thick, scoopable dough.

**3. Chill, roll, chill again.** Freeze the mixture for 1 hour so it firms up. Scoop and roll into balls (about 1 tablespoon each). Yes, your warm hands will try to melt the cold mixture. Yes, this is where your character gets built. Place the rolled balls on a parchment paper–lined baking sheet and freeze again for 30 minutes to 1 hour until firm.

**4. Cover in chocolate.** Melt your chocolate according to package directions. (Low and slow—don't scorch it.) Cover each bourbon ball in the melted chocolate—see Options below— and return it to the lined baking sheet.

**Option A:** Pierce ball with a toothpick. Dip in melted chocolate, spin to cover all over, then let excess drip off.

**Option B:** Set the ball on a fork, and spoon/drizzle melted chocolate over it, then tap off excess. There is no method that involves zero frustration. That's just the ministry of bourbon balls.

**5. Chill.** Once dipped, freeze (or refrigerate) until the chocolate is set.

## Kitchen Tips

- Use good bourbon. If it tastes like regret, your bourbon balls will, too.
- Keep everything cold between steps. If the dough starts getting sticky, put it back in the freezer for 10 to 15 minutes, and regroup.
- If your chocolate gets thick, warm it in short bursts and stir gently.
- Want a little flair? After dipping, sprinkle the tops with pecan dust or flaky salt before the chocolate sets.
- Make Ahead: Roll the balls and keep them frozen (undipped) for up to 1 week. Dip when you're ready.
- Storage: Keep finished bourbon balls in an airtight container in the fridge for up to 2 weeks.
- Freeze: Freeze dipped bourbon balls for up to 2 months. Thaw in the fridge for a bit before serving.
- If you're gifting these, I highly recommend a label that says: "21+ ONLY. DO NOT APPROACH WITHOUT SUPERVISION."

"Sounds like sin. Tastes like Heaven."
*—Luci*

# Chocolate Fudge

**SERVES 36**

**prep:** 15 minutes | **cook:** 10 minutes | **total:** 4 hours 25 minutes *(mostly chilling)*

*Before you clutch your pearls—yes, this fudge has cheese in it. And yes, it is shockingly delicious. It's the kind of recipe that makes people say, "What is this?" and then go back for a second piece before you can even answer. If you're looking for a fancy, delicate, French patisserie moment . . . keep walking. If you want rich, chocolatey, no-grainy-sugar, old-school Southern magic—welcome home.*

**Softened butter, for the baking pan**
**2 (16-ounce) boxes powdered sugar (32 ounces)**
**½ cup unsweetened cocoa powder**
**1 cup (2 sticks) salted butter**
**12 ounces processed cheese product,* cubed**
**Vanilla extract, to taste (start with 1 to 2 teaspoons)**

**1. Prep the pan.** Line an 8x8-inch baking pan with parchment paper, leaving a little overhang for lifting. Lightly butter the parchment.

**2. Mix the dry ingredients.** In a large bowl, whisk together the powdered sugar and cocoa powder until the cocoa disappears and everything looks evenly chocolatey.

**3. Melt the good stuff.** In a heavy-bottomed saucepan, melt the butter and cheese product over medium-low heat, stirring often until smooth and fully combined. (Slow and steady wins the fudge.)

**4. Bring it together.** Pour the hot butter-cheese mixture into the bowl of dry ingredients. Stir until smooth and glossy. Add vanilla, and mix again.

**5. Chill.** Pour into the prepared pan, and smooth the top. Refrigerate for at least 4 hours, or until firm.

**6. Slice and serve.** Lift out using the parchment, cut into squares, and try not to "taste test" half the pan before anybody else sees it.

**I use Velveeta.*

# Easy Microwave Peanut Brittle

**SERVES 20**

**prep:** 5 minutes | **cook:** 9 to 12 minutes *(microwaves vary)* | **total:** 15 to 20 minutes *(plus cooling)*

*This recipe is for people who want homemade candy . . . without committing to a candy thermometer, a double boiler, and a full-on identity crisis. The microwave does the heavy lifting, and you get all the bragging rights.*

---

- **1 cup granulated sugar**
- **½ cup light corn syrup**
- **1½ cups raw peanuts**
- **1 tablespoon unsalted butter**
- **1 teaspoon vanilla extract**
- **1½ teaspoons baking soda**

**1. Prep the pan.** Line a large baking sheet with aluminum foil, and spray it generously with cooking spray. Set aside. (Do not skip this unless you enjoy peeling peanut brittle off your cookware like wallpaper.)

**2. Start the syrup.** In a large microwave-safe glass bowl, stir together the sugar and corn syrup until combined. Microwave on high for 4 minutes. It will boil—don't panic, that's the point.

**3. Remove and add the peanuts and butter.** Carefully remove the bowl. Stir in the peanuts and butter with a heatproof utensil until combined.

**4. Microwave again.** Return the bowl to the microwave, and cook for 5 minutes, or until the mixture turns a deep caramel color. Depending on your microwave, you may need 7 to 8 minutes total here. Keep a close eye on it—the goal is the hard-crack stage (when an instant-read thermometer shows 300° to 310°).

**5. Make it foamy.** Carefully remove from the microwave. Immediately stir in the vanilla and baking soda quickly—the mixture will foam up like it just got the Holy Ghost. Stir just until combined. Do not over-stir, because that foam is what gives brittle that light, honeycomb crunch.

**6. Let it cool.** Pour the foamy mixture onto your prepared baking sheet, and spread it out (carefully) into an even layer. Let it cool completely, then break into pieces.

# Pumpkin Brûlée Tart

SERVES 8 TO 10

**prep:** 20 minutes *(plus cooling)* | **cook:** 40 to 45 minutes | **total:** 4 hours *(includes cooling)*

*This pie is what happens when pumpkin pie grows up. We're talking a gingersnap cookie crust (because we're not out here fighting pie dough), a bourbon-butterscotch-pumpkin filling, and a crackly brûléed sugar top that shatters like glass in the most satisfying way. It's dramatic. It's elegant. It's holiday therapy in a pie plate.*

**CRUST**

- 2 cups gingersnap crumbs (from about 40 cookies)
- ¼ teaspoon salt
- ¼ cup butter (salted or unsalted), melted

**FILLING**

- ⅓ cup packed dark brown sugar
- 2 tablespoons salted butter
- ¼ teaspoon salt
- 1 tablespoon of the good bourbon (maybe even a tad more)
- ½ cup heavy cream
- 1 cup canned pure pumpkin purée
- 1 large egg
- 1 large egg yolk
- Pinch of ground cinnamon
- Pinch of ground nutmeg

**TOPPING**

- ½ cup superfine sugar

**MAKE THE CRUST**

**1. Preheat.** Preheat your oven to 350°.

**2. Make the crust.** In a medium bowl, mix together the gingersnap crumbs and salt. Pour in the melted butter, and stir until the crumbs look evenly moistened—like damp sand that's ready to build a sandcastle. Press firmly into a 9-inch tart pan. Press the bottom first, then work the crumbs up the sides.

**3. Bake and cool.** Bake for 5 minutes, just until slightly darker and set. Let the crust cool completely before filling.

**MAKE THE FILLING**

**1. Make the filling.** In a deep saucepan, combine the brown sugar, butter, and salt. Stir over medium heat until the sugar dissolves, then let it come to a gentle boil. Cook until it turns a deeper brown and smells caramel-y and toasty, about 2 minutes. Remove from heat.

**2. Combine it all.** Carefully stir in the bourbon. It will bubble up—this is normal and also slightly entertaining. Whisk in the heavy cream until smooth. Whisk in the pumpkin purée. Let cool for about 5 minutes (so you don't scramble your eggs). Whisk in the whole egg, egg yolk, cinnamon, and nutmeg until very smooth.

**MAKE THE TART**

**1. Add the filling.** Pour the filling into the cooled crust. Bake until the tart is just set (a slight jiggle in the center is fine— "gentle wobble," not "waves in the Gulf"), 35 to 40 minutes .

**2. Let it cool.** Turn the oven off, crack open the oven door, and let the tart sit inside for 5 to 10 minutes. This helps prevent cracking and keeps the top silky.

**3. Remove and cool.** Remove from the oven, and cool at room temperature for about 3 hours until fully set.

MAKE THE TOPPING

**Torch method** ***(recommended)***

**1. Add the sugar.** Sprinkle ½ cup sugar in a thin, even layer over the top. Don't pile it up—this is a glass shell, not a sand dune.

**2. Torch the sugar.** Use a culinary torch on a low-to-medium flame. Hold the flame 2 to 3 inches above the surface. Start at the edges and keep the torch moving in small circles.Watch as the sugar melts, beads, and turns golden amber. Work inward until the entire top is toasted.

**3. Let it harden.** Let it sit 2 to 3 minutes to harden, then serve for that perfect crack.

**Broiler method** ***(no torch)***

**1. Add the sugar.** Sprinkle ½ cup sugar in a thin, even layer over the top. Don't pile it up—this is a glass shell, not a sand dune.

**2. Cover the edges.** Cover the crust edges with foil to prevent burning.

**3. Broil the sugar.** Preheat your oven to broil. Place tart on upper rack and watch it like a hawk with a caffeine problem. Remove as soon as the sugar melts and caramelizes.

**4. Let it harden.** Let it sit 2 to 3 minutes to harden, then serve for that perfect crack.

## Kitchen Tips

* Fine sugar brûlées best: Granulated works, but superfine gives a smoother glass top.
* Don't torch early. Do it right before serving so the top stays crackly.
* Make Ahead: Bake the pie up to 2 days before, cover, and refrigerate.
* Storage: Keep covered in the fridge for 3 to 4 days. The brûlée top may soften over time—still delicious, just less "crack."

# Easy Lemon Pie

SERVES 8

**prep:** 10 minutes | **chill:** 4 hours | **total:** 4 hours 10 minutes

*This is the pie for people who want something homemade . . . without all the steps that usually come with homemade. I call it Easy Lemon Pie because it tastes like summer and sunshine. But truthfully? It's lemon juice and sweetened condensed milk doing the Lord's work. No oven. No drama. Just whisk, pour, chill, and suddenly, you're the kind of person who "makes pies."*

**LEMON PIE**

- **1 cup lemon juice (fresh or bottled—no judgment, just don't use "a splash")**
- **2 (14-ounce) cans sweetened condensed milk**
- **1 (9-inch) graham cracker piecrust, store-bought or homemade)**

**WHIPPED CREAM**

- **1 cup cold heavy cream**
- **2 to 3 tablespoons powdered sugar (to taste)**
- **½ teaspoon vanilla extract**

**Garnish: lemon slices**

MAKE THE LEMON PIE

**1. Mix the filling.** In a medium bowl, whisk together the lemon juice and sweetened condensed milk until smooth and thickened slightly. You'll notice it start to tighten up pretty quickly—that's the magic.

**2. Pour and chill.** Pour the filling into the graham cracker crust, and smooth the top. Refrigerate for at least 4 hours (overnight is even better if you can stand to wait).

MAKE THE WHIPPED CREAM

**1. Whip the cream.** In the bowl of a stand mixer fitted with a whisk attachment, add cream, sugar, and vanilla. Whip on medium-high until soft peaks form, 3 to 5 minutes.

**2. Dollop and serve.** Dollop whipped cream onto pie slice. Garnish with lemon, if desired.

## Kitchen Tips

- Fresh lemon juice tastes bright and zingy, but bottled works just fine. This pie is not here to judge your schedule.
- For clean slices: Wipe your knife between cuts, or use a warm knife and act like you're on a cooking show.
- Make Ahead: This pie is best made the day before—it sets beautifully overnight.
- Storage: Cover and refrigerate up to 4 to 5 days.
- Freeze: You can freeze it (wrap well) for up to 1 month. Thaw overnight in the fridge.

# I Hate Change

I hate change. Not in a cute, "I'm such a creature of habit" way. I mean I hate it the way a Southern woman hates unannounced company—politely on the outside, spiraling on the inside.

Because change is unknown. And the unknown feels like standing in the dark with your arms out, hoping you don't walk into furniture.

Now, I know people say they love spontaneity. They love adventure. They love surprises. But "surprises" are only cute when they involve a sweet gift from someone or somebody brings you a coffee you didn't ask for.

The kind of unknown that uproots your life? That changes your routines? That makes you relearn where everything is and who you are in a new season? That kind of change? That kind of change will make me break out in hives. Which is why moving was always going to be hard for me—even though it was the dream.

We'd been building a home for three years. Three years. And I know someone reading this is thinking, *Meghan, why did it take three years?* Honey, I ask myself that weekly. There is no reason it should take three years to build a custom home. None. Not unless you're building the Taj Mahal with your bare hands. We were building on our farm—about 25 miles away from the town I grew up in, the town I still did life in, the town that feels like an extension of who I am.

And from the very beginning, I was uneasy. I helped develop the plans. I helped hire contractors. I was present. I was involved. I was the woman with the Pinterest boards and the ideas. But underneath all the planning, there was always reluctance in my heart.

Because even when good things are coming . . . change still feels like loss. And then the building process turned into a full-blown soap opera.

We had a lumber shortage because Hurricane Michael hit, and everybody was rebuilding at the same time. We were trying to rebuild a home in town at the same time we were beginning to build a home out on the farm. We had work shortages, supply shortages, delays, mistakes, setbacks . . . the whole thing was a mess.

If you've ever built a home, I do not envy you. It is an experience I never want to repeat. I have done it once. That is my testimony. That is enough.

By the time we were three years in, the house was almost done—but "almost done" in homebuilding is a cruel phrase. It means it looks finished until you try to live in it. It means you still need last-minute things. Little things. Important things. Things like trim and fixtures and "oh, this entire wall isn't right."

And our second contractor—maybe third, I truly lost count—was not moving fast enough for my husband, Seth. So, he finally said, "We're moving. We'll finish whatever's left ourselves." And I wish I could tell you I responded like a mature adult. But I didn't.

We moved almost overnight—and in my mind, that house was in Egypt. Far, far away from everything I knew.

Like we were relocating to a distant land where I would need a passport and a translator just to find my favorite coffee. And I shut down. I became angry. I became sad. I became the human version of a storm cloud.

I felt like everything familiar was being ripped away from me. I wasn't ready. I felt stuck in the middle of nowhere. I felt like my life had been uprooted—right when I needed stability.

And looking back, I can't believe I felt that way, because this home has been a blessing beyond what I could ever describe. But in that moment? In that raw early season? I couldn't see it yet. All I could see was what I had lost. And then came one of those tiny moments that changed everything.

Three weeks into living in the new house, I drove to Tallahassee to get my teeth aligner attachments off. And if you've ever had clear teeth aligners, you know that day is a national holiday. You get your teeth back. You get to feel smooth enamel again instead of rough little bumps that make you feel like your mouth is lined with plastic blocks.

I wanted to celebrate. I needed a win. I needed something to feel good. Because mentally? I was not okay. I was at my wits' end. I was taking medication to sleep. My creativity was gone. My motivation was gone. I felt like I was watching my own life from the outside, like everything was happening to me and I couldn't catch up. And I know somebody reading this might think, *Meghan . . . a brand-new home and you're falling apart?* I get it.

But here's the truth: The home wasn't finished. We were moving into a place that still needed repairs because of earlier mistakes, and my brain could not handle "unsettled." Add to that the distance from my town, my routines, my comfort—and you've got a perfect recipe for discontentment. So, I'm driving around Tallahassee, trying to go to a little coffee shop near the capitol.

And for some reason, I parked on the backside of the capitol instead of in the parking deck. It was one of those rare "there's a spot right there" moments, so I took it. And the second I parked, a wave of grief hit me out of nowhere.

Because that's what grief does. It doesn't schedule itself. It doesn't knock politely. It just climbs into the passenger seat and says, "Hey, sis. Let's talk." I came apart right there in the driver's seat. Just crying. Ugly crying.

The kind where you're mad at yourself because you have a thousand reasons to be grateful, but you don't feel grateful, and then you feel guilty for not feeling grateful, and then you cry harder because now you're crying about crying.

I was throwing myself a full pity party. And in the middle of it . . . there was a knock on my window. I patted my tears and looked to my left.

There was a woman—early 60s maybe—standing there with two bags: One looked like a medical bag and the other like a suitcase. She looked like she had run a marathon and regretted every step.

She was out of breath. Like, *really* out of breath. I rolled the window down and said, "Hey! Can I help you?" She said, "Hi . . . I normally don't ask things like this . . . but is there any way you can give me a ride to the bus station?"

Now listen. I am not recommending what I did next. I'm not saying you should pick up strangers. I'm saying this was one of those moments where discernment and impulsiveness sat down at the same table and said, "Let's see what happens."

She added, "I'm trying to get on a bus to Spring Hill, and I can't make it. I'm on a new medication, and I'm losing my breath . . . I just don't think I'm going to make it." And something in me softened. Something in me woke up.

I looked her in the eyes and said, "Of course I can take you." Her name was Susan. I grabbed her bags, put them in my car, helped her into the passenger seat like we were old friends, and promised her I'd get her there. I asked, "What time does your bus leave, Susan?"

She wheezed out, "11:55." I looked at the clock. And hollered, "IT'S 11:54, SUSAN!" She said, "I know . . . I'm so sorry . . . I told you I wasn't going to make it." And something inside me snapped—not in a bad way, in a *mission* way.

I said, "NO, MA'AM! I do not accept that. Everything else in my life is falling apart. You ARE gonna make it. I am going to make SURE you make it. We are NOT adding 'missed Greyhound bus' to my growing list of failures."

So, I fly through downtown Tallahassee like I'm auditioning for the movie *Fast & Furious*. I had never been to the Greyhound station before, and of course—because my life is always just a little extra—they were in the middle of moving locations.

So, I'm lost, Susan is gasping, and I'm sweating like I'm the one on the medication. I end up pulling into the bus yard backwards—don't ask me why, it just happened—and buses are coming toward us and I'm thinking, *Well . . . this is it. This is how we go out.*

And the three security guards come running out, waving their arms like inflatable tube men, yelling, "You can't go this way!"

I rolled the window down and matched their chaos with my own. "HEY! I HAVE A FRIEND! HER NAME IS SUSAN! AND SHE'S TRYING TO GET ON THE 11:55 BUS TO SPRING HILL! WHAT DO YOU WANT ME TO DO?!"

They stared at me like they didn't want any part of whatever was happening. And in the gentlest tone, one of them said, "Umm, ma'am . . . okay. You can park right there." Bless them. They chose peace. I parked illegally with confidence, on their recommendation.

Susan tried to tell me she could get it from there. I said, "Susan, no offense, but you are not going to make it across this whole bus yard with less than 15 seconds to spare. I'm taking your bags. I'm running ahead. You just come when you can. I'm not leaving you."

I grabbed her medical bag and suitcase and sprinted across the yard, hollering like a SEC football coach on the sidelines."WHERE IS THE 11:55 BUS TO SPRING HILL?"

The driver—cool as a cucumber—goes, "I'm right here, ma'am." I practically slammed her bags into his hands and said, "THIS IS SUSAN'S. SHE IS COMING. SHE NEEDS A SEAT, PLEASE. DOES SHE HAVE A SEAT ON THIS BUS?" He smiled like he'd seen worse.

"Yes, ma'am," he said. "She'll have a seat." Susan finally makes it over, and she grabs my hands like we've survived something together—because we have.

She says, "I don't know how to thank you."

I (much more calmly at this point) said, "It's fine. You made it. That's all that matters."

She said, "I'm a sweaty mess, but I want to hug you." And I—being who I am—said, "BRING IT IN, SUSAN." So, we hugged. In the bus yard. Like a scene from a movie nobody asked for.

Then she pulled back, looked me right in the eyes, and said, "I really, really hope something good happens in your life." I paused. And y'all . . . I lost it. Because it wasn't about the words. It was about the timing.

It was like God used a stranger named Susan to reach into my self-pity and gently yank me back to purpose. I got her on the bus.

I thanked the security guards on my way back to my illegally parked car. "Thank you for your assistance today." They smiled like I was unwell. Which . . . fair. I got in my car, and I wept. Not the same kind of weeping as before. This was release. This was clarity. Because in that moment, I realized something holy: Even when you're breaking down, at your wits' end, holding on to life by a tiny thread—God can STILL use you.

Even when your world feels like it's shifting under your feet, you can still be a safe place for someone else. And it was like I heard the Lord whisper, *It's not all about you.* Whew. Honestly? I needed that.

Because I had been so consumed with what was changing—what I was losing, what I was afraid of—that I couldn't see the blessings surrounding me. Serving Susan didn't fix my life.

But it lifted my eyes. And that is where joy is found. Not in controlling everything. Not in keeping everything the same. But in stepping outside of yourself long enough to remember why you're here. And then . . . life kept life-ing.

The very month we moved out to the farm, my Mawmaw was diagnosed with terminal liver cancer. And at the same time, our old house—the one I prayed for in high school—was sitting in town. Empty.

And I didn't want to rent it to someone. I didn't want to sell it. I'm emotionally attached to everything I've ever loved. I still feel nostalgia for the car I drove at 16. So, yes, I was attached to a house that held my babies and my memories and my healing.

But my grandparents—my Mawmaw and Pawpaw—were living way out in the opposite direction, far from everything. Pawpaw was still pastoring, still serving, still giving his life away to a small church the way he always had, about 35 minutes away in a town without even a single stop light.

And here's something people don't talk about: A lot of pastors in tiny churches don't have retirement plans. Some folks have mega-church salaries and book deals and budgets. And some folks—like my Pawpaw—have a calling that looks like sacrifice.

Small churches often provide a parsonage while you preach . . . but the day you give your final sermon, the house is no longer yours.

Which means if you've spent a lifetime serving people instead of building personal security, retirement can feel like being gently—and sometimes not so gently—tossed out into the unknown. And then it hit me. Like an epiphany dropped in my lap.

What if the house that meant so much to me . . . could become a safe haven for them? What if the house that held my healing . . . could also hold theirs? Because living in town meant doctors.

Town meant proximity. Town meant help. It meant my Mawmaw would be closer to care, closer to treatment, closer to resources—and closer to me.

So, here I was, the woman who hated change, being asked to live inside it. And then God did what He always does—He took the thing I was clenching my fists around and turned it into an open hand.

We moved Mawmaw and Pawpaw into the house that built me. On Mawmaw's eightieth birthday, instead of a fancy party or a big to-do, the gift was something better: peace. Pawpaw preached his last sermon at that tiny little church in the middle of nowhere—the kind of sermon that isn't just words, but a farewell to a lifetime of pouring himself out. And our family loaded up their life and brought them home.

Not to a parsonage. Not to uncertainty. Not to another "we'll figure it out later." Home.

To a house with history in its walls and love in its frame. A house with no rent payment hanging over their heads. No mortgage. No "how are we going to afford this?" Bills were handled. Burdens were lifted. And for the first time in a long time, they could simply live. Wake up slow. Sit on the porch swing. Focus on each other. Rest. Be cared for the way they've cared for everyone else their whole lives.

And I don't know how to explain the weight of that without crying—how the house I once begged God to give me became the very place He used to give them shelter, comfort, and dignity in the final chapters. How what I thought was mine to cling to became something He asked me to release . . . so it could become a blessing that would outlive my fear of change.

And slowly I realized: Sometimes the very thing you're resisting is the very thing God is using. Sometimes you don't get moved just for you. Sometimes you get moved so you can make room. For purpose. For people. For love.

And for the kind of joy that only comes after you stop fighting the season you're in and start asking, "Alright Lord . . . what are You doing here?"

Because I can tell you this: The season of discontentment didn't last forever. It never does. It passed. And what replaced it wasn't just gratitude. It was joy. Insurmountable joy.

The kind of joy that comes when you realize the change you feared didn't destroy you. It shaped you. It softened you. It positioned you to love people better than you ever could have before. And that . . . is where God was the whole time. Even in the unknown. Even in the move.

Even in the middle of my tears—parked behind the capitol with mascara on my face and a stranger named Susan knocking on my window.

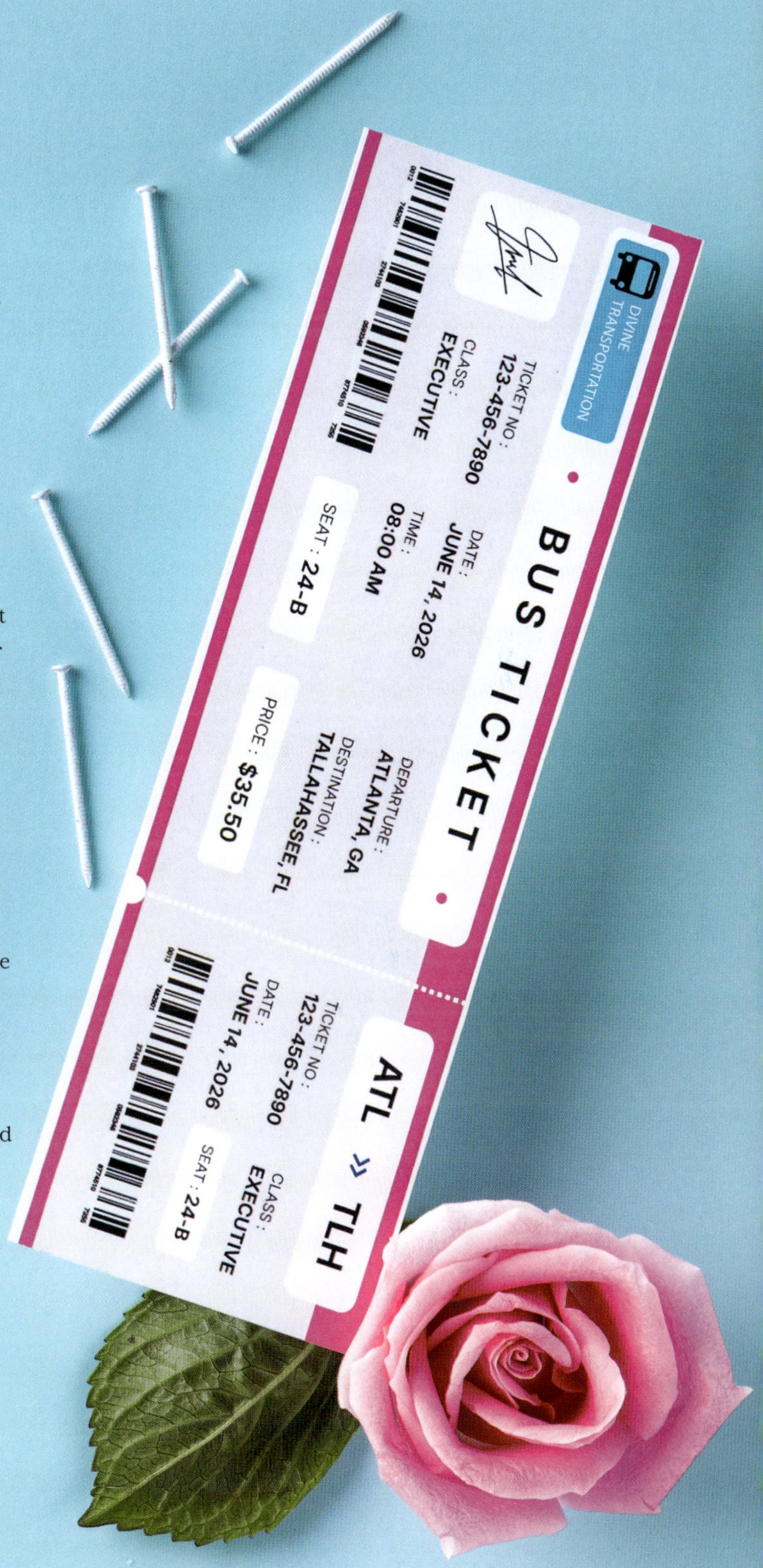

# Peanut Butter Pie

**SERVES 8** *(or 6 if your family is honest)*

**prep:** 10 minutes | **total:** 4 hours 10 minutes *(includes chilling)*

*This is the pie you make when you need something impressive, comforting, and not requiring a single moment of oven-related stress. It's creamy, sweet, and a little crunchy, and it tastes like a Saturday afternoon at Mamaw's house.*

---

- **8 ounces cream cheese, softened**
- **⅔ cup crunchy peanut butter**
- **1¾ cups powdered sugar**
- **1 (8-ounce) tub frozen whipped topping, thawed**
- **1 (9-inch) graham cracker piecrust (store-bought or homemade—no judgment, only gratitude)**

**Garnish: chocolate sauce, chocolate shavings, and chopped peanuts**

**1. Make the filling.** In a large bowl, beat the softened cream cheese with a mixer at medium-low speed until smooth. Add the crunchy peanut butter, and mix until fully combined. Mix in the powdered sugar until smooth and creamy. Gently fold in the whipped topping until the filling is light, fluffy, and completely combined.

**2. Fill and chill.** Spoon the filling into your graham cracker crust, and smooth the top. Cover and refrigerate for at least 4 hours (overnight is even better) until set.

**3. Slice and serve.** Slice and garnish with chocolate sauce, chocolate shavings, and chopped peanuts. Serve and accept the compliments like you worked harder than you did.

# Buttermilk Pie

**SERVES 8**

**prep:** 20 minutes | **cook:** 50 minutes
**total:** 1 hour 40 minutes *(includes cooling)*

*Buttermilk pie is one of those old-school Southern desserts. It's custardy, buttery, lightly tangy, and sweet in a way that feels like home. And if you've never had it before, don't worry—this pie is friendly. She's not fussy. She just needs you to not bring fat-free buttermilk into my kitchen like that's acceptable behavior.*

- **1 9-inch piecrust (store-bought is fine—no judgment)**
- **1½ cups granulated sugar**
- **3 tablespoons all-purpose flour**
- **¼ teaspoon kosher salt**
- **⅛ teaspoon ground cinnamon**
- **1 cup whole buttermilk**
- **½ cup (1 stick) unsalted butter, melted and slightly cooled**
- **3 large eggs, room temperature**
- **1 tablespoon fresh lemon juice**
- **1 teaspoon vanilla extract**

**Garnish: frozen whipped topping, thawed**

**1. Preheat and prep.** Preheat your oven to 350°. Place your piecrust in a 9-inch deep-dish pie plate, and set aside.

**2. Mix dry ingredients.** In a large mixing bowl, whisk together the sugar, flour, salt, and cinnamon.

**3. Mix wet ingredients.** In a second bowl, whisk together buttermilk, melted butter, eggs, lemon juice, and vanilla.

**4. Put it together.** Pour the wet mixture into the dry mixture, and whisk until fully combined and smooth. Pour the filling into your prepared piecrust.

**5. Crust watch.** Bake for 30 minutes. Check the crust edges. If it's browning too quickly, loosely cover the edges with foil. If you like your crust dark and crisp like I do? Let it ride.

**6. Finish baking.** Continue to bake until the center is set with a slight jiggle, about 20 minutes more.

**7. Cool.** Let the pie cool at room temperature before slicing—at least 30 minutes. (I know. Waiting is rude. But custard needs a minute to pull itself together.) Garnish with frozen whipped topping and serve.

# Bourbon Eggnog Bundt Cake

SERVES 12 TO 14

**prep:** 20 minutes | **cook:** 45 to 55 minutes | **total:** 1 hour 30 minutes *(includes cooling)*

*This cake tastes like Christmas walked into your kitchen wearing a velvet dress and smelling faintly of nutmeg. It's buttery, tender, and kissed with eggnog and bourbon—just enough to make you feel festive, not enough to make you start telling family secrets in the living room. Finished with a warm glaze while the cake is still hot (because we're not wasting a single opportunity for flavor), then crowned with a fluffy eggnog buttercream once it cools, she's extra. And she's worth it.*

**BUNDT CAKE**

**Butter and flour, for the Bundt pan**

- **1¼ cups eggnog**
- **2 tablespoons bourbon**
- **1 teaspoon vanilla extract**
- **1 cup (2 sticks) salted butter, room temperature**
- **2 cups granulated sugar**
- **3 large eggs, room temperature**
- **3 cups all-purpose flour**
- **2 teaspoons baking powder**
- **1 teaspoon salt**
- **¼ teaspoon ground nutmeg**
- **½ teaspoon ground cinnamon**

**EGGNOG-BOURBON GLAZE**

- **½ cup powdered sugar**
- **3 to 4 tablespoons eggnog**
- **2 to 12 tablespoons bourbon (This is optional. Your house, your rules.)**
- **½ teaspoon vanilla extract**

**EGGNOG BUTTERCREAM**

- **1 cup (2 sticks) salted butter, room temperature**
- **4 cups powdered sugar**
- **½ teaspoon ground nutmeg**
- **1 teaspoon vanilla extract**
- **¼ cup eggnog**

**MAKE THE BUNDT CAKE**

**1. Prep the oven and your pan.** Preheat your oven to 350°. Butter and flour your 10-cup Bundt pan thoroughly.

**2. Mix the wet ingredients.** In a medium bowl, whisk together the eggnog, bourbon, and vanilla. Set aside.

**3. Cream butter and sugar.** In a large bowl (or stand mixer), beat butter and granulated sugar at medium speed until light and fluffy, about 2 to 3 minutes. Add eggs, one at a time, mixing until just combined.

**4. Mix dry ingredients.** In a separate bowl, whisk together the flour, baking powder, salt, nutmeg, and cinnamon.

**5. Combine.** (Don't overmix!) With the mixer on low speed, alternate adding the flour mixture and the eggnog mixture, beginning and ending with the flour mixture. Mix only until everything is combined. Do not overmix—you want tender and soft, not "brick in a Bundt pan."

**6. Bake.** Pour batter into prepared Bundt pan, and smooth the top. Bake until a toothpick inserted comes out clean (or with a few moist crumbs), 45 to 55 minutes. Let the cake cool in the pan for 10 to 15 minutes, then invert onto a wire rack.

**MAKE THE GLAZE**

**1. Drizzle the glaze.** While the cake is still warm, whisk together the powdered sugar, eggnog, bourbon (if using), and vanilla until smooth and pourable. Drizzle glaze over the warm cake.

**MAKE THE BUTTERCREAM**

**1. Frost the cake.** Once the cake is completely cool, make the buttercream. Beat the butter with a mixer at medium speed until creamy. Add powdered sugar gradually, then add nutmeg, vanilla, and eggnog. Beat until light and fluffy, about 2 to 3 minutes. Pipe or spread buttercream on the cooled cake (I like a pretty swoop situation but do what your spirit leads).

## Kitchen Tips

- Use room-temp eggs: They blend better and help cake bake evenly.
- Grease every ridge like your peace depends on it—because it does.
- Want it bolder? Add an extra tablespoon of bourbon to the glaze, not the batter. The flavor shines more up top.
- Make Ahead: Bake the cake 1 day ahead, glaze it, and store covered. Add buttercream the day of serving for the prettiest finish.
- Storage: Keep covered at room temp for 2 days or refrigerate up to 5 days (Bring to room temp before serving for best texture.).

# The Last Bite

If you've made it to the end of this book, first of all—bless you. That's commitment. That's "I will read a woman writing about bourbon balls, near-death experiences, and grits in the same breath" energy, and I respect it.

But truthfully . . . this book was never just about recipes. It's about what happens *around* the recipes. It's about the stories that live in the ingredients.

The grief that sneaks in while you're stirring. The joy that shows up uninvited—like a free dessert, a front-row parking spot, or a freezer full of ice cream floating in the ocean. It's about the way food has carried me through seasons I didn't know I could survive.

Because life is not neat. It is not measured. It is not always "two cups of peace, one teaspoon of patience, bake at 350° until perfect." Life is more like: a dash of chaos, a cracklin' of disappointment, a glug of courage, and a whole lot of "Lord help me—where is the lid to this container?" Some of these pages were written in laughter. Some were written with shaking hands. Some were written with tears slipping down my face while something was bubbling in the oven like nothing in the world had changed—when everything had. And maybe that's the point. Because even when the world is heavy, you still have to eat. You still have to show up. You still have to feed the people you love—including yourself.

If there's one thing I hope you take from all of this, it's that joy isn't a personality trait you either got or you didn't. Joy is a practice. It's noticing the good when you have a hundred reasons not to. It's choosing gratitude even when your heart is tired. It's serving somebody else when you feel like you don't have a drop left to give—only to discover that somehow . . . you do.

And grace? Grace is what fills in the gaps. Grace is what covers the cake that fell. The casserole that got a little too brown. The season you didn't handle perfectly. The words you wish you could take back. The days you didn't recognize yourself.

Grace is what lets you begin again, with flour on your hands and hope in your chest. This book is a love letter—to my family, to the South, to the people who fed me when I was growing, and to the ones who taught me that a table can be a sanctuary long before it ever becomes a dining room centerpiece.

It's for the ones who cooked with no recipe and still made magic. For the ones who laughed loud and loved harder. For the ones who left us a legacy, not just in stories—but in the way we live

So, wherever you are when you're reading this—whether you're in your first apartment with one pan and a dream, or you're feeding a full house with kids running through the kitchen like tiny hurricanes—here's what I want for you: I want your home to feel safe. I want your table to feel full. I want you to taste comfort. I want you to feel loved.

And I want you to remember that you don't have to have it all figured out to live a beautiful life. Sometimes you just start with what you have. A box mix. A stick of butter. A little faith in the process. And you keep going. Because every meal is a moment. Every table is a gift. Every day you're here is worth something.

So, make the recipes. Call your people. Say what you mean. Hug the ones you love while they're still here. And if nothing else—if everything else feels upside down—put something in the oven, turn on a song, and let your kitchen remind you: You are still here. And you never want to waste that.

Now go on. Feed somebody.

**Buttermilk Ice Cream in a Bag**
Page 47

# Recipe Index

## Something to Get the Party Started



## Something Freshly Baked



## Something Sweet from Scratch



## Something Small for the Sweet Tooth



## Something Extra on the Side



## Something Sweet to Share



## Something to Top It Off



## Something for Sunday Supper

# Acknowledgments

*To my husband, Seth:* Thank you for believing in me on the days I did believe in myself, and on the days I absolutely did not. Thank you for steadying me, cheering me on, and encouraging me to put these stories and recipes on paper. You've supported me through every messy draft, every late-night "does this even make sense?" moment, and every big dream that felt too big. I love you so much, and I'm grateful for all the ways you love me.

*To Braden and Brenlynn:* You two are the heartbeat behind everything I do! You are my greatest joy, my biggest motivation, and my sweetest reminder that every moment in life is worth celebrating—loudly. Thank you for always making me laugh, for stretching my patience, for growing my heart, and for giving me the honor of being your mama. I love you more than words could ever hold.

*To my mother and daddy:* Thank you for bringing me into this world and loving me through every season of it. Thank you for all the ways that you always showed up, for all the ways that you always tried, and for all the love you never let me doubt. I love you both more than I could ever express on paper. I am who I am because of you—both the soft parts and the strong parts—and I will always be grateful.

*To Mamaw, Papaw, Mawmaw, and Pawpaw:* Thank you for loving me unconditionally and for being such a living thread through these pages. Thank you for the prayers, the laughter, the food, the wisdom, and the kind of love that makes a granddaughter feel whole. You didn't just help raise me—you helped shape me. This book carries pieces of you, and I hope it honors you well. I love you all!

*To Tamaryn:* You are my publicist, my manager, my precious Capricorn—the one who keeps my head on straight and my feet on the ground. Thank you for walking with me through the ups and downs of writing this book, and honestly . . . the ups and downs of life itself. Thank you for protecting me, guiding me, and making sure I present myself in the best light possible—even when I'm tempted to show up in chaos and glitter-filled tears. I'm so grateful for you.

*To Joey Retherford:* Thank you for going above and beyond to help me find my perfect "fried-chicken gown" for the cover! You have dressed me for nearly every formal occasion in my life, and you made sure that this particular gown came in quickly and fit me like a glove. Thank you for helping bring our vision to life, for caring about the details, and for making sure this Southern girl got to fry chicken in full glam.

*To Mrs. Vicki Baker:* Thank you for so graciously sharing your Lemon Blueberry Bundt Cake recipe for this book! I was blessed enough to enjoy your wonderful cakes growing up, never knowing that one day one of your recipes would become part of my own story. True to the "Living in the Blessing" story, the Good Lord saw fit to put us in the same room that day, spark a conversation about writing this cookbook, and reveal that you were the baker behind the cake that made that story so special. Thank you for handing that recipe on with such kindness. I am so grateful!

*To everyone mentioned in this book:* They say you become the average of the people you spend the most time with. Well . . . there are more than six of you, and I'm proud to be an "average" of every single one. Thank you for loving me, for encouraging me, for laughing with me, and for making my life richer just by being in it.

*To 83 Press:* You brought this book to life. Truly. Thank you for believing in this dream, for pushing me when I needed it, for guiding me, for editing me, and for loving me through the whole process. Thank you for helping me do something I never thought was possible.

*To my incredible supporters:* It's still wild to me that I get to say I have "fans." I don't think I'll ever get used to that. And honestly, I hope I never do—because one of my constant prayers is that I stay humble and grateful. Thank you for being there on days you didn't even know I was holding on by a thread. I read the comments. I see the messages. I notice the shares. And I feel the love. Thank you for showing up for me in ways I never imagined. Thank you for making this small-town Southern girl feel seen . . . and like she is somebody. From the bottom of my heart—thank you.